# Education for Losers - Memoirs of a Dunce

By

Joe Dullerson

authorHOUSE™
*1663 Liberty Drive, Suite 200*
*Bloomington, Indiana 47403*
*(800) 839-8640*
*www.AuthorHouse.com*

*First published by AuthorHouse 08/08/05*

*ISBN: 1-4208-5334-1 (sc)*

*Printed in the United States of America*
*Bloomington, Indiana*

*This book is printed on acid-free paper.*

# TABLE OF CONTENTS

# EDUCATION FOR LOSERS

At the beginning of 1995 I was languishing in Kuwait enduring the torments of a rotten contract. At the Hawally Education Center the hours of boring invigilation really allowed time for morbid reflection. I looked back over the wasted years as the silenced shouts of Kuwait's tortured echoed through my disturbed mind. I seemed to be doing a permanent runner from the stale joke of programmed existence. "It's been years," said Hunter the Cunter after I'd met him on the train from Carlisle to Glasgow. His acne hadn't improved since 1963. Yes indeed – acned years of nothing at all.

That was the main problem. Life was a boomerang. You started off thinking that life was going to go somewhere but in the end you end up back where you started. You certainly got better at hitting back even if you were punch drunk from all the blows that living threw in your direction. I had started off with great expectations but true to form the fine start crumpled into the ruins of reality. I remember school in Glasgow as a disaster zone where unfortunates were squashed into pliant conformity. You can read all about this in the "Kelvinside Poshboy", a fine piece of narcissist drivel, which completely failed to sell after I'd been conned into wasting £2600 on vanity publishing. I've got piles of the Meisterwerke sitting at home gathering dust. If you fancy a free copy just drop me an e-mail to look at the tale of endless woe. (daviddaworld@aol.com} Maybe after you've read the stuff on the delights of supply teaching and education in general, you may be fired up for more adventures of Joe Dull. At least the latter will give you a taster for the sheer futility of trying to do anything constructive in a world of utter nonsense and garbage. Because the Poshboy hadn't been a success I considered that the world remained a plot to keep me out.

"You wisnae a proper Kelvinside poshboy. I mean whatever induced ye tae drapoot in the first place?" I could just imagine the politically correct sneers coming in my direction. Abstract comment though was right on. The difference between rebellious youth and philosophical mid-life is the way you justify your thoughts and actions. I had made a fetish out of non-commitment, sitting on the fence like a hallucinating missionary. It seemed boring to be carrying round the musty baggage from yesteryear but it was impossible to deny the past. Not that I could advise anybody about anything. I didn't know if people should do this or that – it was all a matter of personal choice and aptitude. The main thing was to stay out of jail and keep the jailers out of your head. Maybe the new century would give me a fresh start? As a pessimist I wasn't expecting a lot. What else can you expect from a Calvinist Scot?

"Aye we'll gies yous a stairt," echoed the voice on the recordings from yesteryear. It would be truly wonderful to know that I hadn't been forgotten in the exciting world of Excess, Excel and Enron. I realized of course that I was an out-of-date boy and always would be, a guarantee that I would never be a megastar. These days, teachers, lecturers and academic types have a low social status if that sort of thing matters to you. But in my idealistic days it had seemed as though intellectual attainment had a clear purpose, even if I still believe that brain power and a sense of humour are powerful survival tools. However you will soon find that back in the classroom nothing has changed since 1960 despite a few superficial alterations to the basic structure. The teacher is still standing in front of unwilling children who don't want to learn anything about the dubious contents of the national curriculum. Even so, the situation today is that the teacher has absolutely no influence whatsoever and is a sitting target for anybody who wants to take a shot at you. Respect doesn't exist anymore and as a teacher, particularly a supply teacher you're on your own. If you cast your mind back to the Bash Street Kids in the Beano you're right on target. The institutional time warp is immune to the passing of the years. In the war of all against all, school messes everybody up. Morons tell you that "you can't draw like this" so naturally you give up all interest in art. "You are not destined to be a Maths scholar" is a comment that ensures failure to become an accountant. The difference between when I went to school and the brave new world of politically-correct education is that the kids are right and the teacher is wrong., hardly a joyous state of affairs. Confrontation exists at every turn whether it is in music, languages and all the rest. There is still a conflict between a liberal arts education and the supposed realism of science and technology. Look for answers in the way you learned the alphabet and how to count up to ten. The people you hated at school in 1952 won't have changed much so you won't want to meet up with them at the class reunion in 2005. Nothing changes at all. You just get older, more cynical and angrier that life is such a con. Nobody could be satisfied with the official programme but that's all there is. Don't believe a word they tell you in the classroom or the staff room. Forget about erudition, praying, knowledge, TV and manipulated insight. All of them are completely useless I can tell you as a supply teacher, management consultant, EFL instructor and general failure. I've tried enlightenment, rebellion, conformity, the all pals act, alternatives, bars and beds and none of them work be assured. There's no compensation or comfort in the emptiness of a demystified universe so why not watch Spartacus again and wonder about the guy on the Cross. Nobody knows anything so don't expect any answers. You'll learn more by jumping out of a plane without a parachute. Teachers need to be total sceptics in order to survive. People seem to imagine that teaching is an easy job with long holidays, compliant students and so on but that's just a tabloid myth.

Having survived school and hating it, I really wonder why I became a teacher. In my family there was an obsession with academic attainment as befitted a strict Presbyterian upbringing. But this was not a valid reason for rejecting opportunities to become a doctor, a lawyer or property mogul to embrace the masochism of the so-called "teaching profession". I was useless at passing exams so I slotted well into the dunce category. Dunces become teachers and I'm both of these. When I was at the Glasgow High School I had imagined that I was a radical hero of consciousness but instead I was an acne-plagued product of the Elmbank Street jail. Nobody ever asked me to join the Former Pupils Club. Due to my incapability to fit in to respectable society I found no alternative to dropping out. I left school with poor qualifications, failed to get into the Army on a Short Service Commission and got a job in 1965 as a van driver delivering paper bags for John Reid and Son of Houldsworth Street, Glasgow. I also failed to get a short service commission in the Army due to "lacking the required spark of enthusiasm"

I wasted five years or so following a career in stupidity with unskilled jobs being the norm. Eventually I got sorted out to some extent and got a degree from Aberdeen University. As a sociologist I was now confirmed as wholly unemployable. I had no prospects. I had opted for the call to the chalk face in a state of delusion that the way forward was in knowledge. Sociology was regarded as a "somewhat vague discipline" so there was little pedagogical future in promoting sociological awareness whatever that might be.

Doing the PGCE at a dismal college in Lancashire wasn't exactly liberation. Subjugation to the System is mandatory in order to complete the post-graduate certificate in education. The Tolpuddle Martyrs had it easy in comparison. No aspiring drop out or mystic romantic could survive the aims and objectives of lesson planning intact. I had thought that the revolution was round the corner, a serious mistake I realized in retrospect. From my perspective in 1969, Western society was the world and CBS was showing the way to *satori* Love and peace were the formula for lasting social change. Drippy delusions notwithstanding, I sincerely believed that "education" was the thing. I took myself too seriously and lost my sense of humour but now I couldn't care less. I made a mistake of major proportions as thirty years of exposure to educational madness has proved. My writing style was messed up by "education". Sure I learned how to use words to some extent and I read voraciously. But, as a spiritual refugee from Being and Time, I couldn't put ideas together or say anything that people would listen to. I felt myself to be a failure from the outset, believing that everything was ultimately pointless. God hadn't worked out nor had the usual panacea – other people. Holy causes hadn't appealed either. The family values lobby didn't seem to merit the moral high ground nor did its opposite. I wanted to be different so I paid the price. *Poenas dare.* I considered that individuality wasn't really permitted in a silly world of team players, good mixers, commitments and being one of the lads. I just wasn't interested in the main stream. Politics too was fundamentally misleading as far as the purpose of life was concerned .So as result of my negative attitude and lack of enthusiasm I found teacher training an uphill struggle. Giving up self-serving Edinburgh hippydom for the banality of Lancashire was a shock to my schizophrenic senses.

I became familiar with state educational jargon, somehow scraping through the minefield designed by government clones to crush all creative energy or artistic initiative. Any positive sides to my personality vanished in meaningless essays on the theories of Piaget as I forgot everything I had learned at university. I argued with the graduate tutor as I objected at every turn to the ridiculous behaviour expected of an aspiring chalkie. I wonder why I didn't stop the process there and then but it was 1975. The universal materialism hadn't quite taken over then and teaching salaries were comfortably above average manual earnings. Little was I to know that as a supply teacher I would be earning less in 2004 than I did in 1990. So much for the all- graduate profession packed out with super teachers. I had got into supply work as I knew that there was no way that I could spend years as a full- time teacher. I managed to get through the probationary year despite the inevitable inspections from County Hall. It was 1976. I'm sure I wouldn't have managed it today with all the draconian OFSTED paranoia and the like. So what? I had to return to my own schooldays to find out why I'd gone right off the rails. Would the years of teaching be an ironic reminder of the misspent days of my youth? Was it the case that I brought to the over-rated vocation an attitude of contempt and derision for any form of learning?

..........................................................................................

# GLASGOW HIGH SCHOOL

I'd been at the same school for 13 years. I passed the entrance exam for the Glasgow High School in 1952 by drawing scribbles on paper. I was asked what this was and informed the Rector that it was a rubbish heap. This original answer seemed to secure my place at this grim selective school ruled by David Lees, otherwise known as "The Dave". He was a man of terrifying aura and austere bearing, despite his five foot nothing. His fluent Japanese and wartime counter-intelligence experience gave him the fearsome reputation that crushed any potential opposition to his Stalinist rule. He gave his staff carte blanche to do what they liked with their charges. Anybody who attended the asylum knows what I am talking about. The school buildings were replicas of a wartime prison camp – A Bloc, B Block, C Block and D Block. A Block was the worst with long draughty corridors exposed to the cold winter winds and driving rain. Here were housed the science laboratories, the art rooms and the ancient lecture theatre where the inmates ate their sandwiches at lunchtime. On the ground floor of A Block there were classic lavatories fitted out in the best Shanks porcelain. I used to watch fat Mole Clark backcombing his slick locks at every interval; his mind filled forever with a reek of old brylcreem. His career as a rock band roadie was assured. C Block was newer but equally grim since on the ground floor Dave HQ was situated, the centre of power, the Rector's Office. Access to the Fuhrer was barred by the steely persona of Miss McClaren, the School Secretary. She wasn't nice like most school secretaries.

Down the corridor from HQ Mr.Paisley's music lessons were held opposite the toilets and near the Primary School Block where I had first been imprisoned at five years of age. In 1960 I was eight years into my thirteen-year stretch in the madhouse. The thundering tones of Beethoven's 9th Symphony had class 1B cowed into terrified silence as Paisley's thick tawse crashed down on the desks. Boys cringed in their seats as the November smog swirled against the windows darkening the sky outside and casting the music room victims into a mood of fear and loathing.

"Who has forgotten their music books?" yelled the sadistic bastard.

Several boys owned up to this unpardonable sin.

"Out here" ordered Paisley.

Hands were held out for a leathering as the rest of the class quaked. Broken spirits shuffled back to their seats.

"Now as for the rest of you" roared Paisley," I don't believe that any of you have brought your books so you are all going to get it, especially as none of you had the guts to admit your guilt".

One after the other the small boys went to the front of the classroom for their undeserved punishment. Fat, effeminate and apparently *nouveaux riche* Archie Hamilton from Newton Mearns held out his obese paw. Alistair Murray, the surgeon's son from Bearsden, half-crazed with repression, gibbered pitifully as the pain of the belt hit his miserable wrists. The back of his hands was already gnawed to pulp as a result of neurotic biting. Next came Kenneth Craig from the deserts of Giffnock, his talent for dropping consonants from key words temporarily curtailed. Carse of Trowan became Arse of Trowan as the Carse vanished in predictable agony. Again and again the belt cracked down on the sweating palms of the miscreants. The wearers of the turd-coloured uniform had no hope of early release from prison. This scene was typical of the treatment meted out by the staff of paid sadists at this supposedly distinguished selective school. Most of them seemed to be ex-forces with strong memories of the war and a liking for brutal discipline. It was only normal to find pupils being smashed into the ground by some psychopathic Sir. Or else they would be doing long ink exercises to satisfy the lunatics who demanded respect from their charges and gave none in return.

"Your incarceration will last forever..."

Yet although most Sirs were bullying cowards there was occasional light relief in Mr.Morton's religious instruction class. Flash Moron was Head of the Combined Cadet Corps and a man of military bearing but a known softie.

"Turn to Revelations, Chapter 6 and make sure you understand the meaning of Judgement" he said.

Bilsland turned to Donaldson and winked. Obviously Moron was leaving the classroom for the more pressing business of organizing CCC field trips. Bilsland's anticipation was well rewarded with Moron saying fruitily…"Now boys I have to leave you for a while so please be informed about the chapter on my return…"

Moron had no interest whatsoever in religious instruction. However it was a compulsory subject. The door slammed and Flash Morton vanished for a smoke with the prefects. Now the class could get on with its main interest – looking at the dirty books distributed round the class by Ian Addison and William McCallum. Soon enough the classroom door opened and the moron flashed in. His face wore a strange expression with his nose wrinkled up in curiosity, Perhaps he knew full well that he had in his presence a crew of little perverts. The class quickly buttoned up and continued the pointless lesson as if nothing were amiss.

The bell went and IB trooped into Nobby Clark's French lessons, which were conducted in broad Glaswegian. Robin Wilson, a church minister's son it was rumoured, settled down to play with himself with his hand up his bright tartan kilt. Wanker Wilson took a lot of stick from tougher, more self-confident boys and today was no exception. Fingers were pointed at him as Nobby's boring voice droned through the dead pages of "Le Francais Vivant".

"*On entre dans le jardin pour ramasser les fleurs*…Right Wilson, is it *la fleur* or *le fleur"*

"Le flower, sir", he muttered quite unaware of the attention he was attracting. The class louts guffawed as Nobby strode up to Wilson's desk to be treated to a view of bare thirteen-year-old thigh and a very red face staring up at him in the utmost embarrassment.

"Don't let me ever see you doing that again!" he thundered as 1B collapsed in hysterics.

Wilson's eyes flooded with tears. Nobby yelled at the class to shut up before asking the wanker to stay behind after the lesson.

"Now look son," Nobby said kindly, having a touch of humanity about him, "You should be doing French and not what you were doing".

Wilson straightened his kilt, adjusted his sporran and ran along to Nobby's "Now run along son…"

This was considerably better treatment than what could be expected from the inferior beings that were the majority of teachers at the dreadful GHS. Case closed till the next one.

The corridors were flowing with boys of all shapes and sizes, all decked out in the turd-coloured uniform. I saw Ronnie Simpson coming towards me. We hated each other. Only the day before we'd had a fight in the electric train just before Partickhill Station. Simpson lived in the grey suburb of Alexandria on the Balloch line and to me was an insufferable bastard whose arrogance was beyond compare. He was a bit like me really although it took me years to recognize this. I well remember the splush of satisfaction as my fist bashed into his nose and simultaneously felt a dagger of pain as Simpson hit me hard on the side of the head. Competition was always present in peer group relationships. Or did I have an inferiority complex, the low self-esteem so beloved by contemporary jargon merchants? Despite all the debate about the causes of one-upmanship Simpson wasn't in the Big League, that motely collection of West End dwellers who took the Milngavie train home from Charing Cross. In the days of the steam train Bilsland and me used to amuse ourselves by throwing copper sulphate crystals stolen from the Chemistry Department out of the train window. We also enjoyed pissing on the walls of the tunnel coming out of Charing Cross. We were revolting. As the train approached Anniesland station shouts of destructive delight echoed round the compartment, which was now in wretched condition, with smashed luggage racks and broken windows. One day we shouted our derision at the greasy porter on the platform. His dandruffed locks and grotesquely pointed shoes spoke of a laughable source of income, plebeian social origins and a working class tobacco habit evident in his nicotine-stained fingers. The porter's view of the grammar school wimps must have been similarly negative what with the turd-coloured uniform, toughtown shoes, satchels, spots and all. Using the language of a proverbial guttersnipe he ran after the train unable to contain his hatred of the posh vandals and spat directly into the compartment. It was a fine sight – spit on the floor, scruffy boys on the seats and stubbed-out wee Woodbines decorating the brown and yellow caps. The disgusting tale continued till the train stopped at Bearsden where the privileged gits climbed through the broken window at the back of the station lavatory. There was no problem about dodging the fare as the Bearsden porter was a sleepy oldster who was blind as a bat.

At the school next day the announcements had a menacing tone.

"The following boys will report to the Office immediately. Talman,Begg,Cameron..."

My friends and I squirmed in our seats. There were sighs of relief all round. These characters were in the Third Year. They travelled on the same train and specialized in smoking cigars in the waiting room while daring an officious prefect to stop them disgracing the good name of the school. The prefect's bluff was called and this time they had pushed their luck too far. A dreadful fate awaited them – suspension at least, possibly expulsion unless they admitted their involvement in deplorable acts. They would of course be hauled up before swinish Piggy Whyte, the Assistant Rector. This was an unenviable experience facing up to his brutal sarcasm. Piggy was Head of Maths and universally hated for his raspberry breath and RAF coldness. It was a frequent sight to see wretched youths advised to "have the grass cut off for tomorrow" – a reference to the modest sideburns that were becoming fashionable. This time though I was safe.

Now it was Daddy Core's gymnastic lessons. Daddy was fat and overblown, muscles gone to seed, a backside slack from exposure to male attention. I'd like to sue this man but he's long dead.

"Right boys. Pants off!" he screamed in the foul-smelling changing rooms.

Boys had to make sure they were not wearing underpants otherwise Daddy's paw would slide up their legs in order to check that they were able to sweat freely. Today it was rope climbing, an enjoyable activity and. Daddy loved every minute of it, all those little boys experiencing the delights of kinetic friction. It was also a revelation to see the other boys' bodies. Some had the most awful acne over backs and chests while faces were mired in boils and pimples. Sykes and his collapsed rib cage were an endless source of merriment and as one of the few English boys in the class his torments were eternal. He was constantly reminded that he had no right to come from Nottingham. A game of madball was being played with lank flabby Kenneth Muir in goal. His effeminate features advertised the lost cause of physical weakness as his large tits flopped up and down in feeble efforts to stop the other side from scoring. Macho boys jeered abuse as goal after goal slammed into the net. However Muir was bright, indifferent to competitive venom. His intellectual prowess at Latin was renowned and strange as it might seem his advanced brainpower guaranteed him protection from persecution. Muir also had other talents such as dexterity in ballroom dancing where he shone at the Cha Cha and the Quickstep. At Warrens' School of Dancing round the corner from the Elmbank Street dump he showed that his ironic sense of humour was highly developed. He must have had well-educated liberal parents I suppose. Who knows?

There were continuing lessons in class-consciousness in these class-conscious days.

The outside society was rigidly hierarchical and life at school was no exception. The classless society hadn't yet reached Sauchiehall Street. Take Michael Massie for instance who had no social advantages unlike myself who had started off with more than a few. He was singled out for particular scorn since he was transparently from the ranks of the Glasgow poor with his third-hand school uniform and pathetic absence of social skills. The aspirations of Massie's deferential parents had not considered the niceties of institutional conformity. School weren't happy places then nor are they now. Genetics is usually in charge with inferior specimens getting a negative press from the surrounding bullies. Massie was fed on a diet of sausages and mash but despite his muscular frame his skin was rarely exposed to sunlight and he appeared to be vitamin deficient. The changing room stank of unwashed bodies. The assistant gym teacher sniffed up the BO as he took off his sandshoe and ordered the goons who had forgotten their kit to bend over. Along with his perverted colleagues such as whisky-faced Jock McLaren, Taylor was an ex-army PE instructor, vilely sadistic and detested by one and all. He bawled out his instructions to "get out the apparatus" as if he was conducting training for unarmed combat for the Great War that never happened. The prevailing culture at the Glasgow High School was that it was ladies played the violin while real men were rugger buggars. Taylor knew all about it.

"TWWAACCCKKK!!" Taylor's meaty features relaxed with pleasure as muttered curses covered up the pain of smarting red bums. The standard black shorts were no protection from the unflagging cruelty of the Physical Training Department. Today these characters would have been up on charges of serious assault but then nobody listened to anybody save the authority figures. Now of course that situation has been totally reversed with disturbing results. Taylor and his cronies were identical in their crippled mental outlook that produced a fascination with humiliation, violence and unquestioning obedience for its own sake. The brutes from Aldershot and Maryhill Barracks were dangerous fetishists, slave to macho mania and the power of unreconstructed masculinity. Even Thoms the school pouf shuddered at the prospect of parading his bare behind in their presence. Poor Thoms knew all about degradation from first-hand experience. Gender definition was even cruder in the stinking 60s.

There was no justice.

"Bums to the wall. It's Homs!" echoed the shouts down dank corridors where bare brick was painted over in institutional yellow and depressing browns. Thoms/Homs had a body shaped like a sagging pear. His eunuch face had long womanly eyelashes giving a fishy air to his soft spongy features. The poor guy came to expect daily mistreatment as the asylum scapegoat. The all-male environment brought out the big guns against anybody who appeared at all feminine. Only a fool would want to be a friend of an alleged poufter unless he wanted to be duffed up by the school Mafia. They made the rules; smashed in anybody they didn't like and were a bunch of unmitigated bastards. I loathe them to this day, more than forty years later. Revolting creatures like David Kerr and Fatty Ferguson dispensed brutal injustice at the drop of a cap. Kerr had an ugly toadish expression on his overlarge face that was similar to a moon landscape. Fatty was an enormous big ape blessed with a purplish complexion and an expression oozing hatred and malice. Nobody seriously argued with these meatheads although sometimes their intimate cronies might put up a token show of resistance to the most distasteful bullying incidents. I trust that these people suffered ample misfortune in later life. The worst swine were made into prefects and as such were sanctioned by the Dave to be as vindictive as they pleased under the pretext of good discipline.

"DON'T ASK QUESTIONS! DO AS YOU ARE TOLD!"

Dirty authority systems didn't suit anybody with an independent mind although nobody seemed immune from the Dave's hit squad. Even Andy Davidson, the smart Alec from Kilmacolm didn't escape their attention. If he overstepped the mark then Kommandant Kerr would be first in with the boot. As the leaders of the school "culture" of threats and intimidation Fatty and Kerr ruled unopposed as members of the School Council. They also had the eyes and ears of Piggy Whyte. Maybe they were just paranoid poleasemen in the making, modern type SS but their existence merely confirmed me in my desire to give conformity a miss. I began to despise the sycophantic posturing of hirelings, the millions of clones who obeyed the inner call of insecurity to keep the major lies going. Liars were everywhere.

"Shiva lives outside the soul,
Kali within the mind,
Only money is their goal,
Life is too unkind,
God is their bore,
Trees hold no charm,
Business is their spirit,
Books list their fantasies".

I knew they were all lying cretins. I'd got a stupid poem published in the school magazine and was asked for comments.

"Ah liked yer poem. It wiz full of intaylectule meaning. Yer a filosofir"

I thought that nobody understood what I was on about, all this gibberish about death being romantic and so on. Romance wasn't in the air as scuffling boys sweating with anger and fear bashed the living daylights out of each other in the playground sheds. The sad sight of broken spectacles, a bloody nose and the shouts of the mob said that life was rotten. Carefully- prepared sandwiches from a loving mother were scattered in puddles. Ripped clothes mocked the concerned efforts of upwardly mobile parents.

"FIGHT FIGHT FIGHT!"

This was the war cry sure to bring the teachers running. The School police were placed on red alert before breaking up the crowd of adrenaline-crazed juveniles. There was a peculiar edge to violence, even if it was upfront and on the level. Aggro was everywhere, to such an extent that it was socially acceptable. Things haven't changed at all. It's just worse with stabbings and assaults a daily occurrence.

At the Combined Cadet Corps parades aggression was the daily norm. Cumming was an unkeen member of the pseudo-army. One morning he came out of school assembly determined not to go on manoeuvres. He had put great efforts into appearing as the worst turned out cadet. His unpolished boots were a disgrace to the Turd Coloured Regiment. His greasy hair flopped over his spotty brow as a symbol of his uncommitted attitude to army discipline. On this fine day he was in revolt, fully aware of the punishments ahead. This was his finest hour, a magic moment when he didn't care a damn. He was long and thin, his face disfigured by moles while his yellowish thatch pretended to be hair. This must have been compensation for his later career as a doctor. He was put on a charge of gross insubordination and then sentenced to guard duty after being marched round the playground in disgrace to the dreadful sound of the bagpipes.

"Cumming. Doghouse. Menzies. Why do you call yourself Menzies? Mingy why do you bother to get up in the morning? Eyes straight. Quick march. You lot are useless. MacPhee, take your hands out of your boots, lad. Spud detail!"

J.C.McPhee "Straight from the Sea". Jack the fish merchant's son and his broad Glasgow accent, business determination on his solid features, his irreverent sense of humour. JCMcP could look after himself when he got lost in the crowds at CCC camp. Then Cumming, Menzies and McP were marched off as the slick looks of Christopher Thompson loomed up. As the School Captain he was at the top of the military hierarchy. He was the worst kind of good boy, a toady excelling at conformity. How did he become so successful at Price Waterhouse? I remembered when he had put on a phoney act with his two fingers shaped in a V sign, his throat producing burping sounds as he tried to be one of the boys. I wasn't convinced with his cop routine, as I'd had plenty of experience of the Captain's pious outlook when I'd entered for the Dr Hutchinson's Chemistry Prize. I wasn't good at Chemistry but wanted to escape from the pointless lessons such as those directed by Picken, an insensitive clown who taught Latin. I objected to Picken's existence as he relished tormenting and upsetting pupils. My father had even gone into see the Dave to complain about my mistreatment. I  had had a bad time with the swine after being continually belted by the sarcastic Latinist for failing to learn verb declensions properly. So it came as a bit of a respite to be sitting behind the Captain. But Thompson wasn't going to allow any copying or allow me to cheat in the examination. The Captain had sternly covered up his paper kyboshing my efforts to subvert the examination system. Without a hope of obtaining even 5%, it was all a laugh for me. I wondered if the Cap was going to grass me up to the invigilator but nothing happened. I still cursed him as the biggest shite since the dawn of defecation so pleased by the outcome of a false alarm I handed in my paper, delighted to have failed once again. Thus my perspective on assessment, testing and general measuring of talent or ability was more than influenced by such incidents.

Because his father was a School Governor, a so-called friend of the School, Chris was eventually appointed Captain and his brother made a prefect for no other reason other than parental influence. Who wouldn't be sceptical about democracy and electoral procedure in such circumstances? Chrissie the cissie was flawless with hair parted in model style. He exemplified school perfection. He was a shining example of the daily observation of the School Rule Book. No wonder I hated him and all that he represented. I wasn't unhappy that we didn't meet up at the class of 52 reunion in Glasgow. I'm sure there would have been very little to say.

There was never a dull moment. Spike Campbell, a French teacher who looked like and acted as psychopath came into the dining hall to remonstrate with Bill Barclay. Spike was a big thug, much disliked but Bill was equally thuggish and a hardened troublemaker who had no qualms about taking on Spike.

"Fuck off Spike!" Bill spat as Spike attempted to break up a fight. The Spike grabbed him and the two of them hit out wildly before the languages bovver boy gained the upper hand. Bill was dragged off to the Office for a dressing down.

One fine day there was a riot. A wonderful sense of exhilaration swept over the school. Certain of ultimate victory some resourceful boys had taken over the tannoy system to air their complaints.

*"Break free from your jolly jails. Be unafraid to die then you'll never want to hear another or hate your mother far inside where nothing is and no rule was ever made…*

It was a revolutionary broadcast based on gut reactions to totalitarian control. The school revos were storming the reality studios in truly heroic fashion without a thought for the consequences. When their names were discovered these boys would not be coming back next term. However for a moment an air of belligerence put all other considerations in abeyance. From the windows of the Geography Department in C Block a wall map was hanging from a pair of trousers, the property of some wretch debagged in the toilets. A car had been manhandled into the playground with dustbin lids tied to the bumpers. Paddy the Geography man was its owner who angrily demanded that his precious possession be removed forthwith from the playground and carried up the steps to Holland Street. To a chorus of derision this was done as the crowd turned its attention to the scene being enacted outside the Office. Piggy was standing there accompanied by the Dave. Both were wearing dusty old black gowns, the emblem of chalky bossmen, but today they signified nothing more than dirty dishrags. This was their school and Steerforth himself would have been proud of their stalwart declaration in defence of the propertied rights of men. Old Beaky Leach from the Latin Department scuttled past to amused grins. Beaky was liked – a great honour. Nobody would bother him. His rambles through the pages of Paterson and McNaughton were famous studies in oratory characterized by Beaky leaning forward over the front desks of the classroom as he spieled off his fascinating memories of school life. This performance was a classic still from Tom Brown's schooldays. Beaky's classroom was near the Office so he was liable to random visits from the Dave. Also it was opposite the Prefect' Room where kangaroo courts were held. Beaky loathed unpleasantness or aggression as he shuddered with distaste at the distant shouts of intimidation.

Then as suddenly as it had started the rumpus died down. Boys eagerly discussed the dramatic events of the day. Who had put potassium permanganate in the A Block water system? Who were the instant media stars who had broadcast the message of uprising? Nobody would ever know why I hadn't made it to the Former Pupils Club.

In his dismal Chemistry Lab M'Grunt looked up from his Bunsen burner, which was brewing tea. M'Grunt's long face spoke of an impending early death from lung cancer. His strong Glaswegian accent spoke from an industrial crypt. His lessons were dull and repetitive, consisting mainly of tedious note-taking and laborious experiments. The class favourite was Wilson Blakey, a little tick who listened attentively as the results of the latest incomprehensible test were read out. I looked out of the windows thinking of the vast slave camp that was the city of Glasgow. There was the sad feel of the shop floor in December as M'Grunt's funereal tones drilled a message of industrial doom into my protesting brain.

"As expected...top, Blakey. Well done, Wilson. Second, John Adams, third William McIntosh...now down to the flops at the lower end of the scale. Bennet 30%. Treymaine 16% and as for you Dullerson, just take it away will ye?"

After I had come bottom of the class M'Grunt had taken me aside.

"Ye ken ye caun dae better than this," he said.

I cried pathetically, struck to the core as Uncle M'Grunt urged me to try harder. The last thing I wanted was for my father to find out how poorly I was doing as Prof.Dullerson held high hopes for my future. It was a major tragedy that I wasn't an academic high flyer. Not that there were any reasons for optimism as my last report had been a shocker, bottom of the class and marked down as a useless waster. It would take me years to see through the arbitrary nature of marking schemes and the meaningless aspects of examination assessment. Still, I was somehow inspired through my mist of tears to pull my socks up. If I did well in M'Grunt's future tests then surely I too would be able to work in a school science department, make tea on my personal Bunsen burner and teach crowds of dupes about the Halogens. I would be able to inspire brilliant scientists by enthralling generations of boys with the mysteries of the Permutit Process, the importance of the molecular weight of the inert gases and the role of calcium carbonate in the manufacture of soap. I envisaged the fascinating life of an ICI reject model as a downmarket chemist clad in a vomit-brown lab coat. Such a fate seemed uninteresting to say the least, almost as absurd as ending up as the unfortunate Doc.Low who seemed to be committed full-time to the General Gas Equation and the vagaries of the Archimedean Principles.

Despite being a proper Physics teacher Doc's lessons were renowned for weak discipline, fatal when trying to deal with stroppy kids. Lee Wypers was an established anarchist who was sure to raise jeers all round by producing mayhem. Weights and balances went flying in all directions as all uncertainty principles were refuted in the definitive results of experimental failure. Wyper's overbearing presence guaranteed major unscientific fiascos as noxious fumes filled the laboratory and broken test tubes lay scattered on the floor. He was a natural comedian in any situation, a calculating loudmouth who knew exactly how to produce chaos. He was famous throughout the school.

Science seemed to be insane with its objective posturing, mechanistic illusions and the ever-present factor of human error. I used to watch Jim Twill, another Physics teacher, talking about convection currents as he blew cigarette smoke through a series of glass tubes. Jim sported a luxurious Professor Jimmy Edwards moustache and wore a pearl tiepin. He enjoyed practicing his gold swings in the staff room along with a shot of Glen Grant. I thought these activities were much more interesting than imparting the nonsense in the textbooks. But as a result of his hopeless teaching most of his pupils were predestined to fail their exams. It was just the same in Mr.Reilly's Physics test when I came bottom in an electricity test with 1%. I was incapable of understanding the meaning or relevance of voltmeters, rheostats and convoluted circuits. I didn't fit the male stereotype with a fascination for technology in general. I must have been a lady as defined by the bastards in the PE Department.

So rather than worry unduly about academic success it was much more rewarding to have a belly laugh listening to Wypers' mocking voice. One day he had done a magnificent job in destroying Mr.Smith's Maths lesson. Smith was a new teacher of obvious inexperience with an acned face and a voice from the end of the world. He was an immediate spotty object of scorn.

"Now boys, a bit quieter please". His dead, squeaky delivery failed completely to control the rowdy members of the class.

"Hand in your ink exercises ", he continued feebly. Ink exercises were considered to be an important part of coursework.

Lee Wypers and Dougie Hope looked at each other.

"We wiz at a party last night, sir" scowled Dougie in his heavy Glaswegian accent.

"Isn't that right, Lee" he howled, looking over to Wypers who was enormous at 22 stone.

"Aye that's right, sir. Dougie's right, sir. Him and me wiz out winching".Wypers was openly mocking.

Smith was in a helpless rage.

"Right. Out here Wypers and hold out your hand. If you don't then I'll take you down to the Rector," bawled Smith at top volume. The belt swished down cutting air as Wypers pulled his hands apart, dropping the exercise book that had been placed over his wrists to prevent possible bruising. Smith made several more attempts to belt him properly but again Wypers pulled the same trick.

"Wypers, come down with me to the Office immediately!" Smith had lost all of his limited cool.

"Right sir, I'm coming sir" Wypers said insolently.

"Are you coming, Dougie?" he smirked at Dougie as he wandered nonchalantly towards the door.

"Naw. Not yet. Lee. Gie us a kiss, Lee" jeered Dougie as the class rioted.

At the door Smith's nerve snapped and he ordered Wypers back to his seat amidst uproar. This was a common event and not so long before Smith had totally lost control of a class and had to be rescued by Piggy Whyte. Piggy had brutally belted the class into submission to show who was boss, to the eternal shame of Squeaky Smith, the pox-ridden insult to the memory of Pythagoras and Euclid. Wypers was irrepressible. He was a star who shone in total insignificance.

In Mr.Mortimer's geography class he was causing more trouble.

"I am awarding you a "U", Wyper for completely unsatisfactory work and conduct," said Mr.Mortimer in his clipped RAF English, mispronouncing his name to gales of laughter. It was as if Major Bigglesworth had turned to stone as Wypers smirked in oafish satisfaction on hearing of Mortimer's low opinion of him. It was quite an achievement to be rated "U" at the bottom of the attitude and application stakes. School reports followed a system of "diligence marks" which seemed a fairly useless method of character analysis and were wide open to misinterpretation. A "U" though was reserved for particularly anti-social behaviour and outlook. The diligence marks ranged from the following:-

Top of the tree was "E" (outstanding in ability and initiative)

This was seconded by S+ (works beyond native ability and exceeds expectations)

Then there was "S" (works within native ability and the bounds one would expect)

Lower down the scale was "S-" (fails to work within perceived bands of ability and expectations and requires marked improvement)

The "U" was beyond the pale (completely unreliable and unsatisfactory)

Wypers lived up to his reputation in class after class. It was laugh a minute when he was around. A classic performance took place in Zombie's Religious Instruction session when Wypers was called in to assist Zombie in his exercises in jovial sadism. Zombie taught French and like most of the teachers had no time at all for any sort of religion. He took pleasure in insulting the Talmud since the Jewish boys were absent and took every opportunity to ridicule the Bible. He was a Nikita Khrushchev double act with a shabby suit and shaven head. Like his look-alike hero, Zombie was a master of the absurd who enjoyed producing the most ridiculous situations. Aping the mad Russian at the United Nations he banged his shoe on the desk promising to bury the lot of us. He then imitated the SS in the Warsaw Ghetto as he matched Wypers the largest boy from Glasgow against Sykes, the smallest boy from Nottingham. Wypers read out some biblical passage from Revelations suggesting that men shall seek God but will not find Him. Doom and damnation were inevitable according to the Wypers prophecies. Then Sykes countered in wavering tones promising Paradise to the believing worthy. The class tensed with excitement at the spectacle of a bear baiting a mouse. Sykes was castigated for his Sassenach origins while Wypers was subtly praised for being an obliging minder. Zombie smiled like an SS General observing religious leaders debating religious teaching before going to the gas chamber. Zombie's God was in Thyssen's accounts department as he mocked the word of God.

"Well, clearly we're all doomed" he jeered as he wrote up a summary of the lesson

"Arbeit macht Frei" Did Zombie deserve an "E" for such an original approach to whole class teaching?

Certainly I thought that the diligence assessment exercise was flawed since it was a matter of personal opinion on the part of the teacher. I was lucky not to join Wypers in the disgrace stakes as my geography book was in a similarly poor state to his – covered with badly drawn diagrams and maps splotched with ink blots decorated by messy writing scattered at random over the pathetic pages. I could have done with some modern assistance in the form of computer graphics. I was less enamoured by the neat presentation of work and much more interested in Mr.Mortimer's tales of entrepots and his South American adventures. According to Mortimer he and Mr.Fairweather had worked their passage as stevedores to Montevideo and had visited Caracas, Buenos Aires and Rio de Janeiro. Both of them were of course experts in Mayan history and had climbed Popocatepetl twenty times. It was racy stuff. Fairweather had taken over my mind in the Primary School where I endured three years of his regime from Primary 5 to Primary 7, which fluctuated between rigid authoritarianism and liberal fun and games. He was reputed to be a "psychologist" since he gave sociometry tests and unorthodox lectures in perception. Lay opinion at this time regarded "psychological methods" with suspicion. More than once his secular attitude to religion had produced an angry reaction from my father who had a Presbyterian Rock of Ages standpoint. As a leading elder of Wellington Church in University Avenue he wasn't going to accept a rational approach to spiritual matters, particularly from a source of dubious social origin. However I did feel that my father had a sort of grudging respect for a teacher who was unafraid to be true to his principles. Years later I had some e-mail correspondence with Fairweather. His sardonic tone seemed much the same while he seemed unaware of how much he had affected his pupils.

After yet another sociometry test David Marshall and Alistair Murray were seen crumpling up bits of paper into their desks. Ashen-faced they were ordered by the psychologist to reveal the contents. Murray and various nicknames and here he was being addressed by Marshall as the Helly Buggar in a filthy note. You could just imagine the Helly Buggar giving snails for spiders to eat and then drowning the poor creatures in boiling oil.

"Dear Helly Buggar…I live at 7 Shit Street, Pissville. There is a stink of jobbies and unclean toilets."

One look from Fairy and the game was up. Marshall was petrified. I remember him as being tall and slightly effeminate with long hair flopping over his forehead. He abhorred violence.

"Please sir?" his voice broke. Fairy looked down quite indifferent to his pathetic pleadings. He smashed into Marshall's hands with his thick belt. Hitting a nine-year-old boy in such a way was beyond the pale but in those days nobody complained. Soon Marshall was back in his seat sobbing quietly. He deserved much better along with poor Murray who was the next to have his hands bashed to a red pulp. Fairy then continued to read the results of his little questionnaire as if nothing had happened.

When I mentioned this incident to Marshall more than forty years later he had no recollection at all. His opinion was that Fairweather was the best teacher he ever had and that it was best to leave things that way. He wanted nothing to do with anybody from the Glasgow High School and refused to allow his personal details to be published for the brochure produced for the Class of 52 Reunion. Maybe he was right to maintain his state of denial, as reliving this time would have been too painful. I knew that many people who had attended the school never forgot the bad times they had experienced but at least they were prepared to talk about them.

Fairy read out some more answers.

"The most popular boy is…." The most popular boy beamed. "The boy on whom I could rely to lend me money is …." The Shylock at the back of the class rubbed his hands together at the prospect of more business. And so on. Even the punishments practiced by Fairy were bizarre.

"Stare at that dot, boy!" Fairy ordered Hosie to focus on a dot as he covered the blackboard in thousands of dots.

"Count them, Hosie!" commanded Fairy after Hosie had come in late with the fanciful excuse that his dog had died. Although this was probably true, nobody believed him and the class had burst into mocking laughter. Only the day before Hosie had been pulled up short for writing a bad essay on "My fried dog" rather than the correct version of "My friend's dog".

A likely story, Hosie!" bellowed Fairy as Hosie was set to his impossible task. This was trial by ordeal.

"Dot,dot.dot,dot,dot,dot,dot,dot,dot,dot,dot,dot,dot…" the victim lost count at the fifth dot or so, his powers of concentration vanquished by absurdity.

"Dull dull dull dull dull dull dull dull dull dull……

Damn damn damn damn damn damn damn damn

Damp damp damp damp damp damp damp damp

LLLLLLLLLLLLLLLLLLLLLLLLLLLLLLL
Bell bell bell bell bell bell bell bell bell bell bell
Hell hell hell hell hell hell hell hell hell hell hell........"

Fairy's voiced droned on as the weary hours of childhood wasted away.

"Milngavie is the centre of European civilization. When I was shovelling coal in Rio de Janeiro after climbing the Andes with Mr.Mortimer I realized that when Popocatepetl last erupted way back in 1664 this was clear indication to me that there was only one focal point in life, the nothingness of the dot."

What all this was about was anybody's guess. Jeremy Kidd evidently didn't think much of the world when he blew out his cells with his father's service revolver. Apparently he suffered from "psychological problems". Everybody did. After his death had been announced I regretted the first fight I had had with him, one of the half dozen or so that I experienced at school. Life was one big psychological problem surrounded on all sides by assorted lunacies. At that time I could never understand what anybody *felt* about anything, There weren't any emotions apart from anger, scorn, pain and resentment. I was introspective and puffed up with immature conceit as I struggled to protect myself from the "orders are orders" poison gas that was suffocating us all at the GHS. We were being crushed into pliant conformity by the relentless sledgehammer of mindless discipline. There seemed to be no escape and no choice as the authorities had got it all taped due to the success of their obedience propaganda initiative. In conjunction with the teachers's union, the Educational Institute of Scotland, the Dave and his crowd of quislings made it clear that nothing was open to negotiation. You did something because you were told to do it. Uh Huh.

"This is the authorities speaking. Do not attempt to resist. All opposition will be ruthlessly crushed. The thought police are a moral force...."

Life in the Primary School had been pretty depressing. It suffered a reign of terror under the tyranny of Mr.Rankin, an extremely tall, thin, stern man who seemed able to reduce boys to whimpering ruins at a glance. Alistair Murray was once in his class. He was an easy target. Unfortunately for him he found himself in daily situations of the utmost humiliation. After a rumpus one day Rankin asked all the "funny men" to come to the front of the classroom. Hector Cameron and his cronies had been giggling. Nobody volunteered for execution so Murray was singled out for ridicule.

Daft Murray tried desperately hard at everything he did but his attempts were invariably in vain. He always came bottom of the class in spelling tests, even after hours of laborious work. Murray was a born victim who was a monument to the meaning of suffering. His face cracked into floods of tears as Rankin's sarcastic tongue lashed out. Rankin was a swine, an apostle of moral farce who savoured his bloody tests of helpless anguish and suffering.

"If any boy wants to join a greeting session, " he snarled, " he can come and see me any time". Rankin scowled nastily at the thought of yelling at a crushed group of snivelling boys in school shorts. This man should not have been allowed to retire to enjoy his old age in peace but it's too late to bring charges now.

Strange to think that school started off with such high hopes. I remember my father insisting on brushing my hair so that it was parted in the middle and plastered down both sides of the head. This hairstyle was a symbol of the goody goody, so I used to mess up my hair immediately after I had escaped from the car each morning. It was only Gordon MacMillan back in Primary One who could match me in the presentation of a perfect image. He and I were Miss Nina Logan's pets in the autumn of 1952 and usually at the top of the class. The grooming for academic distinction continued with Miss Jackson in Primary Two, Miss Turner in Primary Three and pint-sized Miss Barrie in Primary Four followed by the three years of brainwashing with Fairweather. It was a long haul of wailing and gnashing of teeth. There was the sad tale of Malcolm Livingstone coming in with his mother sometime in 1953 to tell the stunned class that his house had collapsed in a landslide. I believe Malcolm is still functioning somewhere in the education system of Northern England. Then there were those who had got away from the school mindblower such as Ian Dickie who emigrated to South Africa. John Graham preferred to stay and wet his breeks during the Arithmetic lesson. Fatty Graham cried his eyes out as he was told to go to the toilet and clean himself up. Mrs.Newton, the school nurse, general dogsbody and busybody gave out harsh, carbolic sympathy to crowds of little boys in their brown shorts and blazers. After school I invited my friends round to tea at my house in University Gardens, W2.

I don't suppose I would have anything in common now with Lorimer Gray, Angus McIver ,Archie Orme or Alistair Murray. Would they remember sitting around eating rock buns before "Listening with Mother"? No listening with father then.

"DINGDADING. Are you sitting comfortably? Then we'll begin.."

Education for me had begun back in 1951 at Dean House Nursery School where I learned how keen I was to work and what a fluent reader I was. Dean House was situated back from Great Western Road and run by a Mrs.Brand. Dean House was a step on from the University Baby Club where my brother and I were sent in order to learn to behave with other academic offspring from the W2 neighbourhood. We weren't the most sociable of children, rotten mixers in fact, who were proud of our anti-social tendencies as we bullied unmercifully other children who were invited to play with us. The usual scenario was of parents in other rooms while we tortured unwilling guests like Michael Stubbs or Stuart Peebles. We would pretend to welcome the poor swine so as to assure visiting parents that all was well. This early toilet training stank of the worst aspects of Schadenfreude, guaranteeing future decline and fall

With all this sort of background disturbance and ongoing persecution it was hardly surprising that in days to come the Helly Buggar ended up in a special school for dumbheads. It was astonishing that his special needs had not been recognized, let alone catered for, but in 1957 you just did what you were told. In later years the news was he managed to find a job in the catering industry, that refuge of misfits where he was condemned to enjoy yet more insult and vilification. The HB didn't make it to the Senior School where the environment was much rougher than the primary set up. It came as a shock to be exposed to hardman Dotty McNab, a nasty Maths teacher who crammed meaningless mathematical information into young skulls. In contrast to Squeaky Smith McNab knew the score and didn't tolerate indiscipline. His lessons weren't fun. He talked way above the heads of the majority so was able to produce a class average way below 50% in his Algebra exam.

"Now if x to the power of n becomes transmuted to the power of n qua infinity then it is axiomatic that x has no definite value. The transmogrification of x as an absolute is then dialectically apparent." McNab lectured to thin air. I couldn't understand what he was talking about. Bennett the dunce didn't have a clue while by now I had wholly lost interest in mathematical imponderables and hoped merely to avoid Dotty's harsh words on my feeble efforts.

"This is disgraceful work. You are not destined to be a maths scholar" he leered.

His breath stank of shit.

So nothing could be worse than to come from Primary School brilliance to be revealed as a thicko in the mayhem of the Senior School. The joy of calculus and dy/dx, the arithmetical side of geometry along with an insight into applied mathematics would never be mine. I saw myself as yet another casualty of the narrow-minded Scottish Education Department with its narrow focus on a rigid adherence to unchangeable curricular boundaries and a fixation on subject independence. Later on I would come up against the bureaucratic inflexibility of the SED and the Scottish General Teaching Council. Meanwhile it was reassuring to know that success or failure in life depended on academic culture and the whims of your average domine. If you were told that you were incompetent then you naturally agreed with this insane message. All that mattered then as now was passing exams even if you were driven crazy in the process. It took me years for me to learn more worthwhile lessons such as realizing that effective survival required reliance on independent thinking. Back then I was still a mug, unstreetwise, an ineffectual liar, easily led and an obvious candidate for a career as a waster. It was no easy peasy.

Next-door Willie Wilson was struggling manfully against overwhelming odds. There were hoots of pity as he mentioned that he had paid £995 for a house in Lenzie (a fair amount in the early 1960s). Boys comfortably insulated from the harsh world of economic reality thought that anybody without the readies had somehow failed as a human being. Clearly Willie was missing out somewhere. Schoolboy success stories like Andy Preston certainly thought so. Andy was a beery horror story of a juvenile delinquent who took pleasure in flaunting his family's brassy wealth. He drove into school in a Mercedes as soon as he had passed his driving test. His fat mug leered at the dusty masters drawing up in battered Morris Oxfords, riding tacky Vespa scooters or else tying up the doors of rusty Ford Consuls with bits of string. Fast lane Andy looked askance at the graduate bums on campus, these cretinous pedestrians who were crawling along in Slow Street, Quite so. Elmbank Street had never seen anything like it, all these displays of youthful affluence. The Dave strongly disapproved of such arrogant posings and made consistent attempts to encourage pupils to arrive at school in less opulent style. I was in a double bind myself as my father used to drive my brothers and myself to school in a tiny Renault with the Rolls left at home in the garage. I could never understand why he did this, especially when as children we had been brought up to see ourselves differently from the rest of the world. Probably it was merely to save petrol as the Renault hardly illustrated membership of the Elect. Even if God helped those who helped themselves my father wanted to keep his superiority complex in the background. This was a disturbing form of schizophrenia somewhat at odds with the GHS motto of "Sursum Semper"(always on top) – a missionary position that told me that Jesus didn't love me either. As I jabbered through the old tapes of my memory I almost welcomed the exclusion from the Old Boys Register, proud to be regarded as a renegade. But I wasn't as bad surely as Ed McLintock ?

"Hey boys, I killed a woman last night. Stupid bitch got in the way of the wheels. Stupid bitch. Ha ha, I'm out on bail" He was laughing his head off. His uncle was at the University and while he was away Ed had stolen his car for a joyride. Ed was 16 and thought to hell with it all. He wanted to destroy. Careering wildly down the road in Pollockshields he approached a zebra crossing, crashing into the unfortunate woman, killing her instantly. Next morning Ed was a hero. He was lucky to be given only two years for this crime. He wasn't bothered about death and broken necks and didn't give his uncle's wrecked car a second thought. Ed valued his public image as a wide boy much more than the life of some irrelevant pedestrian. The smart Alec approach got full marks, an approach that was vital in dealing with the heavy daily purgatory. Boys needed to act up to each other and I was no exception since everything was geared to becoming a Big Shot. It was essential to establish a tough and independent image even if you had little idea of self-preservation in the face of universal authoritarianism. I used to cringe inwardly if the psychological sponge cake that was my personality was challenged. It wouldn't have been that difficult to pull me apart once people got through the pseudo-sophisticated façade to find an obvious drip. Maybe it was the same for everybody.

There were plenty of image merchants about. Tony McBride slipped into his seat. Smooth Tony had a knowing look on his Italian-Jewish features. Only last night we heard that he had been out with Andy Preston in the Merc picking up girls who were willing and able. All the women at that time were aping Christine Keeler and Mandy Rice-Davies. Tony did the male bit with his heavy Stephen Ward sunglasses. His voice was carefully modulated to sound as mid-Atlantic as possible in the fashion of the time. He was as American as the best of them from the West of Scotland. No doubt he and Andy had been cruising around till 4 a.m. but no sign showed. His carefully manicured fingernails gave him the air of a Mafia made man. I thought he could easily have been from New York with his air of urban panache, his strings of women and entrée to what I naively imagined were extremely sophisticated nitespots. I wondered enviously how many women Tony had had but maybe he was still a virgin for all I knew. Still, Tony seemed to be the sort of Lucky Strike figure that would get away with everything and appear perfectly legal. He was an operator in a world of undone ink exercises and illicit button-down tab collars. Early on it was apparent that mixed genes had different characteristics. Semites and Shalom boys from showbiz were clever flash boys, cosmopolitan sharpsters and driven by a callous market intuition. I admired them but was obliged to act out a Nazi charade for the sake of the anti-Semitism that permeated the school like a bad smell. The Elmbank Street dump was polluted by a sick view of the chosen race. Michael Karter's fist slammed into my head as I fell with a terrific thump on the hard playground. I'd been winning till Karter cracked me a smart uppercut that knocked me out. I'd failed hopelessly to prove that I was head and shoulders above the rest but perhaps there would be another time to get my own back. Karter looked like a Syrian secret policeman and was of course a "10%-er", that is one of the Jewish boys who made up 10% of the school population. They were generally regarded as agents of the Sanhedrin working for Shin Bet or Mossad. The ignorance of world history and the redneck racism of Scotland at that time were appalling and it showed. Rabbi Cosgrove was responsible for the spiritual welfare of boys from the Judaic religious persuasion. He had to deal with a parochial antipathy which expressed itself in most of the school setting themselves up as self-styled Waffen SS. Boys thought it was pretty smart to indulge in a spot of Jew-baiting. Memories of the tragic times in the Warsaw Ghetto and the death camps were revived by the GHS gentile propaganda machine via the tacit support of the hierarchy.

"Jewish boys are exempt from statutory religious requirements " the Dave informed the school assembly to the sound of sniggering. The school chaplain, Rev.John Gray or Pope Gray as he was known looked on stony-faced.

"Jewish boys" continued the Dave" would make their way to Garnethill Synagogue where they have their own activities." The Dave bored on about the Hebrews who stood out as hooknoses but the GHS Nazi Party was an amateur bunch. Rabbi Cosgrove's brood were much wiser and more worldly-wise than the silly parochialists who shouted out their ignorance of world history.

"Hey Jew boy. Howie Clapham.Clap Clap. You got the clap.Whit ever happened to the Israelites? Yer a shite Stan. Stanley Shapiro.Yid bum Jew. That's my boy. Very nice material"

I remember the look of angry rebuke on Shapiro's face after he had been insulted. I felt ashamed as Kommandant Oberstumfuhrer Kerr led a chorus of abuse. He was delighting in the fear showing on the faces of the circumcised. However there was no Krystallnacht and the real pogroms stayed in the eternal flame at Yad Vashem. The Thousand Year Reich also had a low profile at the end of the day. I looked over at Steven Grossman, a dark swarthy cardsharp who looked like Stevie Wonder. Grossman seemed far removed from the puerile values of the Glaswegian nowhere where one was supposed to know one's place. Steven wasn't bothered about respectability's empty glitter but he knew all about the casino – Anastasia's brilliant invention. He understood money and business, knowing that it was cash that counted. At 17 he had already made piles of dough at chemin-de-fer, roulette and straight poker while there was always his sideline at the racetrack to help things along. Steven was part of an extended community that shut out all the nonsense of the Elmbank Street Der Streumer.

Aaronson would no doubt be a successful doctor, Sam Silver a rich lawyer while Bernard Wasserstein would of course be a well-known academic. Paul Zederbaum was swarthy, overweight and at the age of 14 looked at least 24. He spent most of his time in La Ronde, a sleazy café with darkened windows somewhere in Sauchiehall Street. I would watch enviously as Charles Woolfson, Jerry Miller and David Gordon met up with Sharon, Miriam and Esthen from the Westbourne School for Girls. Sadly I wasn't in the competition since the Levantines had wrapped everything up. It seemed easy for them as they seemed to know who they were and were part of a social network that would support them in anything they chose to do. I was a white Presbyterian boy stuck on an isolated pedestal of my own. I was confused about who I was and felt removed from any sense of pretending to belong. I acted out my part of failure on cue.

At the school sports I raised a cheer by coming in last in the half mile, a quarter of a mile behind the other competitors. I was out of synch stuck in another space between worlds. I wasn't sure if I hated the impending tidal wave of modernism and its déclassé philosophy or if I was stuck in some stuffy past. I declined advice from anybody and decided to go my own way and to hell with the consequences. I was good at producing problems for myself but I had to rise above the years of conditioning by rejecting the GHS message that academic failures were failures per se

To me the stalwarts in Elmbank Street were hopelessly stuck in an old newsreel with the doors of perception stuck in the gormless pages of the Scottish Daily Express and the Bulletin in Albion Street. The prejudices of these rags were ludicrous, their editorials raving on about the danger of the Church of Scotland being taken over by Catholic priests. If I had been running the Glasgow 1960s then the whole show would have been closed down after one night. There was nothing swinging about the city on the bonnie banks o' Clyde. Andrew Neill, the well-known newspaper man, went to Paisley Grammar School so did he know any better I wonder? The point was that things continued against all the odds – even the miserable Sursum Semper. Campbell-Bannerman and Bonar Law might have been distinguished old boys way back in the old days but times had changed. Any fool could see that the great ideals of Liberalism had been decimated by the dismal decades of the lousiest century of the lot. The land fit for heroes to live in was a stale pipedream remembered only by the ghosts who were members of Elgar's fan club. The past only lived on in the pages of the School Magazine. I reached 1937 where there were obscure references to some character called Mr.McCallum acting out Virgil. The land fit for dafties to live in stared out of the erudite pages that were stuffed with merry anecdotes, obscure aphorisms and pithy social comment. I looked at a frozen fantasy, a 1910 still from the Winslow Boy. The words from the school song “To those who follow after to fill the place they fill” were a yawning disappointment. I dreamed up some off-stage jeers and a suitable exeunt. The league of scholastic gentlemen was out of style as was the turd-coloured uniform, blazer and badge. It was astonishing that there were any survivors at all.

Back in 1B Bilsland was scribbling on the desks of Mousie Morrison’s C Block History classroom. Mousie was a miserable bastard with a face straight out of a Dracula film.

“Get on with your reading “ he ordered grumpily as he taught History in his unique way.

Bilsland looked up from his illicit art. “MOUSIE IS A CUNT” was etched neatly on the wooden desk. Proving that he was just that Mousie took out his belt and gave Bilsland six of the best. Bilsland crumpled before being dragged down to the Dave for a repeat performance, Later Bilsland appeared white-faced and trembling, cowed into silence by the power of the Lochgelly. I was glad to hear that Bilsland had done his duty a few years later by getting expelled for being drunk and incapable at the School Dance. Well done Al.

The thing was that at the Glasgow Grim School you got a PhD in the negative side of living. Your were stuffed with recipes for rejecting the whole nonsense of good citizenship which was designed to keep you bloated forever and ever, Some of the more sensitive souls found it all a bit hard to take.

Bobby Corbett was affectionately known as Choo choo due to his trainspotting hobby. He ran about the playground with Ian Shankland who believed he was Thomas the Tank Engine. Bobby wore NHS spectacles and an expression of deep unhappiness. With the tank engine he seemed to be suffering from retarded emotional development.

Maybe he wasn’t but the general atmosphere of Protestant gloom didn’t help people to express themselves. Bobby and Shankland were similar to James Cook who was tormented by bullies. Delicate flowers were treated very badly and daisies were trampled underfoot. Somebody spat in Cook’s face, a quite inexcusable act since James was quite inoffensive as his shocked look of rebuke testified. Also calling him “Plook” was ludicrous as his skin was without blemish but the name stuck. He was good at music, playing an advanced form of classical piano and therefore the darling of Harry M’Gill the Head of Music. Harry was a soft and sentimental sort of man, destroyed by living in an age of total philistinism and the tyranny of the mob. He should have been the Head of Music at M’Gill University in Canada where his life would have been much easier. Harry went through purgatory trying to interest the GHS yobs in Mozart, Beethoven and Handel but without success. There was too much competition from Duane Eddy, Del Shannon, Connie Francis, the Miracles, the Shondelles and the early Beatles. Harry had no control at all, a tragic persona and one of the world's lost causes. However, he had considerable talent as he took responsibility for putting on the annual concert and directing the competent school orchestra. Along with his unpleasant henchmen Messrs.Bolling and Paisley, Harry did a great job earning himself a permanent place in the annals of Sursum Semper. What a wonderful sense of occasion was in the air at the School Concert as there always was at all important school function. Tanhauser boomed out in St.Andrew's Hall along with the singing of the Junior Choir, the dignified singing of the School Song and God Save the Queen. Harry, Bolling and Paisley were toffed up in their best tails.

"O Alma Mater Glorious..." began the school song as the words choked in my throat. I saw the pompous prefects strutting up and down the aisles, ushering parents and friends to their seats. The Dave had the place of honour in the middle of the balcony surrounded by sycophants and lackeys. I could see the snotty Colonel Thompson and Mrs.Thompson deep in conference with the Office Fuhrer. I despised them all, the prefects especially with their mad badges decorating their turdish blazers, the Dave and his Politburo, the whole empty show. I sneered at the shoddy dignitaries flowering away in faded fancy hats, Giffnock uniforms and the self-satisfaction that comes from living in Troon. All had come to say hello to Mr.Paisley's dramatic orchestral style. He conducted with a long lock of hair falling over his brow, wearing a pair of shining patent leather shoes and the stiff dress shirt that covered his sweaty torso. He and Bolling were competing for the position of Chief Drama Queen while Harry M'Gill was recognized as the driving force behind the musical throne. Paisley's grasp of the acciacatura was impeccable as his pristine vocal interpretations of the choral peaks rang from the St.Andrew's rooftop. Here he was this Paisley, a man quite wasted by his own estimation, done in by thwarted ambition but no doubt still aspiring to be the Head of Music and Entertainment at the BBC in Queen Margaret Drive. He would make sure that the Scottish National Orchestra knew all about his genius.

"SCATTERED BUNCHES OF THE AMBITIOUS MEATHEADS, BUTCHERS OF THE GRASS AND GREEN...LABORATORY GROCERS TRADING SHRIVELLED LIVES FOR TIES AND SQUASHED AMBITIONS.."

Then there was majestic inspiration and veritable spring-cleaning of the mind as several unsavoury characters slipped out of the front row of the bass section in the choir. It was time to start misbehaving and act against the huge rulebook that controlled every aspect of life in the Scotland that existed in my head.

"A spring-cleaning of the mind" intoned the Rev.McBore at yet another Scottish church service on yet another Sunday morning in Scotland. I fought off my guilty conscience as the lure of alcohol took over any reservations I had about breaking parental taboos on the dreaded drink. To hell with spring-cleaning I thought as I met the boys out in the street. Lachie, Cumming, Campbell, Fraser and Hughes were all ready to get into the boozer. First we had to avoid the prefects. Eyes right. Eyes left. Eyes straight ahead into the first pub. Vodka and limes all round with gut-wrenching pints of heavy on top. We all threw down the alcoholic filth down our parched throats.

"What a howl all this is, boys. Did the Dave see us going out? Oh cripes, we'll be forrit in the morning".

Then paranoia as outside the pub we bumped into the prefects who were bound to smell our beery breath. The bunch of shits would be sure to call us into the Council Room the next day to make us account for our crimes. The evening scene faded to the sounds of "Land of Hope and Glory". Next day, one by one, the drinkers shuffled into the Council Room for a humiliation session and forced confession all round to the School Police. As usual I muffed my lines and admitted to everything. Dire consequences followed with a visit to the Dave. Although it all seemed very serious to me at the time with alcohol being the main reason for my disgrace, the Dave was pretty friendly towards me. Maybe he was more understanding than I realized.

"If you tell your father, all will be well, " he said. But I didn't dare reveal this latest offence as I had just had a terrible report that I had signed myself. When it eventually came out that my father hadn't been informed of my disgraceful report with its forged signature or my reprehensible conduct at the concert I knew that Hell was waiting to gobble up another sinner. I quaked in the old man's study as the dreadful prospect of social ostracism from correct society loomed.

"Unless you show an acceptable degree of contrition you are going to be down the road," my father informed me grimly. Angst bounced off the study walls as it was made plain that the Predestination of the Elect did not apply to fools like me. I had initiated an impossible conflict between biological determinism and the bleak facts of social circumstances. I could see that my reward for such heresy was a rotten life below deck in the Merchant Navy and early death from peptic ulcers. Bad vibes were everywhere I looked so it was hardly surprising that I went into free fall. I could sympathise with my father's reaction of course but he was out of touch with seventeen-year-old perspectives and I had to be myself regardless. It came as a surprise to me that life in other families was less regimented, more ordinary and less controversial. Kenny Fraser's family for instance seemed more relaxed and informal. Religion was lacking in his enigmatic personality, he who was the imaginary protégé of Sydney Greenstreet and a disciple of anarchist folklore. He was knowledgeable about how people were, the attitudes they projected as a result of social conditioning, that sort of thing. He enjoyed late breakfasts, greasy kitchen and a half a dozen pints of Guinness at noon. When he was fourteen he turned up on Sports Day at Old Anniesland looking very mature in the company of his parents who obviously allowed him to dress and behave as an adult. I wondered about the meaning of maturity after that. Kenny had an older brother called "Prof" who had a talent for languages and radical opinions after a spell studying in Moscow. Fraser lived in his brother's shadow and was a successful failure as an imaginary organization man.

"If I'd been running the company there's no doubt that I'd have taken a more detailed interest in the personnel department " said Kenny as he helped himself to a Sobrane Black Russian cigarette. He was the complete armchair entrepreneur who was well able to justify the lackadaisical outlook that contributed to his lack of university degree, despite seven years of indifferent effort. In his dry and cynical tones he would wax sentimental about life's ifs and maybes. He talked about people he'd known at school.

"Langmuir used to drink down at the Arlington Bar but he got tired of the idiotic pish that people talked. We saw a lot of each other before but he wouldn't pay for a carry out last night. He got into a fight so I left him in Woodlands Road. He should have stayed till closing time. "

I thought of Langmuir's decadent alcoholic face. Where was Langmuir now?

"I don't know how you'd get on with Campbell" Kenny said to me. " He hasn't changed really". He poured himself a short.

"Times pass, people change," he sneered at the flat in Grosvenor Mansions in Observatory Road just off Byres Road.

I thought back to the times when I used to wander the school corridors with Kenny and Campbell. We pretended to be on some important errand for a member of staff. We looked highly suspicious together so we were bound to be picked up for questioning.

Dotty McNab had apprehended us on the way out.

"Where are you going?" Dotty asked in mean and condescending tones.

"Rugby practice, sir" we lied feebly. This was a poor excuse really as none of us had even sniffed the 12th Fifteen. Next morning an announcement came ordering us to the Office where Piggy Whyte belted us viciously. We had been caught red-handed without a proper excuse. Holding out our hands for a lashing felt very degrading and we were seventeen years old with no possibility of getting our own back. Can you imagine such a scene today?

So the secret of success lay in getting some good pals who identified with the problems that arose from non-conformity. My friends and I were rebellious lunatics, a menace to Ralph Nader and his unsafe at any speed rubbish coming across the Atlantic. The speed controls of the 1965 Act brought in the 70 mph limit. This seemed to be one of the biggest disasters since the 1832 Reform Act that had eventually resulted in morons of all sorts having the vote. However the limit didn't stop McCann killing himself in his Lotus Cortina somewhere near Blanefield outside Glasgow. The roads of the West of Scotland were one big racetrack, they weren't that crowded and there were no speed cameras to plague would-be speed freaks. Tom Maloney's customized Rover 105 terrified the life out of more sober motorists. He drove it like a police car on a chase. Driving was a great buzz . If you were young then the biggest thrill in the world was driving as fast as you could. It is just the same today. It takes quite a few years to get out of the habit and I was no exception. These days of course I am a model motorist but not in 1965 when I used to borrow my father's Zodiac. I'd take the day off school to indulge my addiction to speed. All I was interested in was a mad burn-up. One day the Zodiac was packed to capacity as the boys and me pushed the clock over the ton on the Drymen to Balmaha road. The Zodiac was an unwieldy machine with a 3-speed column change but it had a powerful 3-litre engine with an overdrive. I have no idea how we survived our crazy drive on what is even now a narrow country road. I didn't care at the time and driving to the limit was much more fun than listening to my father yelling at me.

"You'll kill us all!" he screamed as I pushed the Zodiac up to 60 mph somewhere on the Maryhill Road one Sunday after church. I wanted to prove that I was as good as Jim Clark, Jackie Stewart or Stirling Moss. I thought that I could drive fast and remain in control. The only thing to do to have access to the Zodiac was to have a duplicate key. At that time all you had to do was to walk into the nearest accessory shop and buy a replacement with no questions asked. I did this with deviant glee. All went well for a while until one day I landed myself in hot water. I drove up the drive at my home hoping that my father was out but to my horror there he was in the garden beside the summerhouse enjoying the afternoon sun.

I could only silently hand over the keys and endure his entirely justified rage.

"You're useless!" he yelled. "A waster and a sinner going rapidly downhill. You'll have to leave home as your mother and I have had more than enough of you. There's no chance that you'll even smell a university."

I wondered at this reference to the odour of academe. The smell of musty tomes was hardly attractive to my philistine inclinations. And so it went on – a nightmare. Temporary respite came from spending as much time as possible away from home. My friends were less than welcome as my parents regarded them as a bad influence. As I came from a teetotal household I made sure that my pals were drinkers and as unlike my family as possible. I really am surprised that I didn't get into a lot more trouble than I did since I was so reckless and self-destructive. I came across alcoholic households where cirrhosis of the liver was more than likely. I met fat dads who ate steak and prawn cocktails and mothers who were living examples of advertisement women. Near Kelvinside Academy playing fields at Balgray there were plenty of modern G-plan dreams to choose from. I liked the idea of futures founded on the bevvy, get-rich-quick plans and television conditioning. Up the road there were dragster mechanics drooling over Jaguar XK 150s.

"It'll do a ton and a half on the straight " they enthused.

So the rich computer geeks of the future spent their weekends burning up rubber on Loch Lomondside. It seemed a great way to live even if I didn't have any money.

Some people though weren't up to scratch. Take Cumming for example whose best shot was revving up his mother's Hillman Minx out to the Allander pub at Milngavie. As usual the only place to go was the pub but his lager-induced driving style was a joke. A standing start at the traffic lights didn't amount to much in a British Leyland rustbucket. You had to aspire to be a Le Mans 24-hour world champion to be anybody. All of us were mockers to a man and this was before John Lennon who was asked if he was a rocker and replied that he was a mocker. Real men were heroes like Fangio, Jackie Stewart and Colin Chapman who could probably drive the Millia Miglia flat out with their eyes shut. Characters like Cumming were crawling along with the back markers in first gear. Unfortunately though world recognition was slow in coming. Instead of taking the pole position at Le Mans we were driving out to Blanefield in Bilsland's untaxed old Austin 10. We flew round a corner near to the Helly Buggar's house where a cyclist was standing. We were pretty pissed. A bottle smashed into the side of the car as Bilsland screeched to a halt. The cyclist was threatened with dire retribution as he vanished into a nearby wood. We ran around drunkenly to no avail. Next thing we knew was that we were all being arrested for disorderly conduct and breach of the peace. Police cars were everywhere with cops in hot pursuit of the GHS yobs.

"Right, Alec" said a fuzz. "Get the Big Wan". Down I went as I was frog-marched in a half-nelson with the others into a squad car. It was all very dramatic and unexpected. At Milngavie police station we were all interviewed, cautioned and told to go since we had been wearing the turd-coloured uniform. One of our party also happened to have an uncle who worked as a detective in the Maryhill Division. So we walked free. I considered that we'd done nothing wrong save make a noise. Apparently the reason we were picked up was because this particular country road had been the scene of "incidents". We were just an addition to the statistics. Later a letter arrived through the door at home from Stirling and Clackmannan Constabulary, the heaviest outfit in the West of Scotland. Before I had the opportunity to intercept it, my father had got hold of the letter that informed me that if anything of a similar nature occurred in the future then serious repercussions would follow.

"This is clear proof that you are for the high jump," my father said in angry despair.

I wasn't much of an athlete though and would have to learn fast. This was what education had done for me so far. I had got absolutely nowhere and had brought shame and failure to all and sundry. My guilt was profound and began to realize that life is full of regrets.

"THIS IS THE POLICE. YOU ARE UNDER ARREST.YOU ARE NOW IN POLICE CUSTODY.YOUR LOCAL POLICE KNOW BEST. REPORT TO YOUR LOCAL POLICE STATION IMMEDIATELY.ADVICE WILL BE GIVEN THERE ON YOUR CIVIL RIGHTS".

"Just sign on the dotted line on the charge sheet, sir. All the paperwork's been taken care of. Look forward to seeing you in court with your guilty plea, sir." The desk sergeant handed out a free pen with a government logo.

..............................................................................

# THE IVORY TOWER

At one stage education seemed to be everything and the mystique of the university had me spellbound. Yet years later after expressing deep intellectual insights into the nature of the copula, the meanderings of Ethnomethodology and the total confusion of semiotics it became clear that academic pursuits were useless in obtaining a decent salary. I saw no point in continuing the massacre of language with an MA in Linguistics. So it took me a long time to understand the obscurity of most academic endeavours but in the 1960s students were enjoying a lurid reputation as social revolutionaries, artistic innovators and radical bohemians. I was a student with the required long hair, beads, bangles and I listened to the Beatles. This Renaissance was breaking all previous records in the 20th century repeat. Along with nameless others I saw myself as a visionary head, a style of being that implied vast inner awareness that was greatly assisted by selective drug use. This image suited my mental state of total withdrawal and my inability to relate to anybody or anything save in a gormless intellectual way. Despite my pitiful income I was happy with the romance of student existence and had no regrets about dropping out just at the right time in my life.

It was 1969.Ross Barnett waxed forth on the mysteries of experience, which were axiomatically based on the interpretation of observation. I envied my brainy associates at Oxford who were acting out the reincarnation of Herman Hesse and the Steppenwolf. I had an unjustified inferiority complex about Ross and his charmed life at Queens College. He seemed to be extremely sophisticated about pop music trends and the political meaning of acid groups such as the Grateful Dead who were somewhat shocking. The sounds of Crossby, Stills, Nash and Young were on the same deep, exalted level as Deep Purple. Ross was tall and thin who was destined to be a Professor of Philosophy from day one.

"I applied myself to the task of reading the book ten times before I was fully able to understand what the author was on about" he said.

His rapier intellect showed a profound knowledge of Wittgenstein putting into the shadows my humble explorations of definitions of mental illness. I was in thrall to the likes of R.D.Laing and the acid guru Timothy Leary who advised everybody to" tune in, turn on and drop out." It seemed pretty sensible advice all things considered as the official trip was going nowhere. I wondered though why Ross studied "scientific philosophy" and why Wittgenstein would want to write out hundreds of propositions for undergraduate indigestion. The young Ludwig must have been a real madman to give away the family inheritance to lose his way in endless paradigms precariously balanced on swinging blocks and pulleys.

I came across Ross and Gat who were deeply involved in a discussion on the semantics of the Triumph of the Will. I felt antagonistic to their reasoned arguments and affected rational discourse, mainly because I was expecting to be exposed as an intellectual embarrassment when it came to the crunch.

"Now Heidegger is really a fine fellow," said Ross with conviction.

"Exactly, man, just like Cohen Bendt, another fine fellow along with David Frost and Che Guevara", replied Gat absurdly.

The word "fine was a cliché over-used to describe the positive qualities or such and such a person. As a great image merchant myself I thought that I was pretty fine myself with my leather jackets, long naval coat, pink cravats and stupid Woodstock grin. Howyadoin man? Fine, thanks, fine just fine. I'm fine. Yet it wasn't so simple according to Ross.

"Yes what Heidegger is saying here at this moment in time is that Hegel's metaphysics fails to make significant philosophical impact, in the hermeneutic sense, on the earlier existentialist dimension delineated by Kierkegaard. We can find a connection in this respect with the a-tonal approaches utilized by Stockhausen in his experimental musical propositions."

Stockhausen's awful sounds blared down from the speakers. The heads sat around the hi-fi system getting into the sounds. Gat for one was absorbed in "seeing " and "feeling", an apparently revolutionary development in the psychology of the senses. It was important to experience everything lectured Ross.

"Getting into things is everything " he went on as Pink Floyd took our minds spiralling through a kaleidoscope of competing definitions and meanings from which any conclusion was permitted. Ross seemed very much in control with his slightly wrinkled forehead and the eyes behind the granny glasses set in a suitably sardonic expression.Gat was talking knowledgeably about the new culture.

"The new culture needs no reliance on first principles as the axiom is fashionably dead. The rich tradition of classical construction on the other hand cannot be ignored by blind devotion to Bauhaus architecture. You can see this phenomenon in practice with Fellini jeering at the world through Gore Vidal's smile. The film "Roma" turned an unseeing eye to baton-wielding police smashing up the latest anti-war protest by the nice boys and girls at the international school."

The rich nature of the experience wandered into an infinity where the end was nigh. I reflected on my new tailor-made yellow shirt with its large collar, my tight, shiny blue trousers and the strikingly trendy Cuban heel boots that I had just purchased. I had discarded my unfashionable pinstripe suit since I saw myself moving in the opposite direction to the beery accountants and dull fatties who ran the world. At least as a student I was free of the time-wasting nonsense of earning a living although I disapproved of student demos and didn't really like alternative music. As the room swam in circles I felt ill at ease. I was a late arrival to the world of thought for thought's sake and was unfamiliar with dope consciousness – although anything was better than alcohol. Dope hadn't done much for me in the past when I'd smoked the odd joint. However there didn't seem much harm in cannabis even if possession of the laughing gear was regarded as a serious crime. Students anyway had bought the anti-consumer message where a bit of blow brightened things up no end. The way forward was in knowledge and not in a personal loan account. I was pleased to be a self-made subversive acting out the part of the average Rolling Stone reader. So I found myself in the company of two intellectual poseurs whose only contribution to further understanding of the world was vague speculation on imponderable projections. But I was just the same.

"Itatness comes from San Francisco where the most amazing things are happening, things to make Dale Carnegie turn in his grave" enthused Ross.

I wasn't quite sure what this instant fad line signified although I found the mystic attractions of the Hills of Bhutan fairly exciting. Mysticism as such enjoyed a high rating in some student circles and I was a mystic and a dreamer. There was no itatness at Marxist brainwashing centres like the LSE where students were mainlined into economic truth. Even if most things boiled down to business at the end of the day, I preferred to ignore disturbing issues and the nefarious workings of capitalism. The hippy dream was sacrosanct.

I could hear the voices of the superior critics in the background.

"There is deontological significance for Bohr and Einstein in the astrophysical interpretation of enharmonic chord structure. What is really happening here is the philosophical definition of the recording studio's master creation, that is the rock star syndrome." Ross was on a roll.

"Quite so, man " Gat stroked his black moustache. " And politically of course Vietnam is the catalyst of the New Dawn. Take Jimi Hendrix the cosmic revolutionary from Queens."

I protested that all this stuff was the living contradiction of the American media machine. These media products just happened to have the vocabulary to put themselves into perspective. Hollywood is still the centre of the star system that produces commercially viable attitudes. I suggested that it was better to look to Europe where European film directors like Jean Luc Goddard were more in touch with social issues. I surprised myself with my forceful delivery, which naturally failed to impress the poseurs who were thundering through the Dark Side of the Moon. I was all pretentious impression management.

"Real and actual problems affecting life on the planet are best left to the people running the system " preached Ross in true copout mode. "There's no point in being addicted to regression". He laid down the establishment line as all academic philosophers are supposed to do.

I didn't really believe in the rosy pictures produced by the rock industry. Frank Zappa mocked that you got nothing with a college diploma. He might have been right although up to date I had found less than nothing with my lack of training or qualifications. I looked at the copy of "The Psychotic" which was beside me. What was psychosis? I was fired by a burning purpose to expose the nefarious purpose of official psychiatry and plastic gurus like Zappa. I imagined that bullshitter like Zappa were typical examples of system people, artistic Uncle Toms who had sold out by recommending the benefits of being "far out as long as record sales stayed high. I was a real puritan/ As an Uncle Tome or Uncle Tome I saw myself getting into thought processes despite being clueless about which ideas were worth a punt. Existence had too many contradictions that were outside analytical limitations. Once I got to university I began to live the halcyon days to lose myself in a major rewrite of the fraudulent Freud, part of the contemporary attack on behaviourist psychology. Life certainly improved without having to fall in and out of the ghastly pubs. As a serious man of letters I knew where to go, given that there were "head" and "straight" pubs. This was a stupid scene where my stupidity found expression in a creepy leaning towards moral detachment. I had fallen under the spell of"sociological neutrality" and its promise of "value freedom" I envisage miraculous solutions to life in general but instead of finding Nirvana I'd analysed my utopias into a pompous thesis on the Mafia's role in American politics. I was a system man myself as I came to realize when I had written to the "Scotsman" on the presumed issues of the day. My righteous utilitarian tones spoke of the reasonableness of compromise, democratic debate and the importance of keeping within the law. This licker's manifesto produced no reactions whatsoever showing me that I was completely out of touch with the "now generation" who were supposed to be radicalising the universe.

Clearly there was no mileage in proposing the greatest happiness of the greatest number or the banning of student demonstrations. I was still an out of date boy.

There was no escape really. The New Age was just another sales line while Western individualism was a barrier to progress in the new world of psychochemical spirituality. The uncharted voyages into consciousness were more likely to produce brain damage than any profound insight into the meaning of life. There were far too many boring punch lines on the uniqueness of the self – a sure indication of American influence. Ultimately it seemed that the reprogramming of the self was founded on political naivety and silly assumptions that all human beings possessed the same metabolism. It was nonsense to state that your were yourself and nobody else as a final goal. So my Union Corse version of the cosmic connection illustrated armies of psychic cheapsters more than willing to masquerade as cosmonauts or spiritual adventurers. It was hard work blowing away all these illusions as I was clueless which shadows danced on which walls. Moral philosophy wasn't up to much when it was reduced to rote-learning the creaky gurus from Athens who didn't measure up to the new consciousness popeyes. I discarded Socrates and Pythagoras since I was tired of total immersion in lines of print. I dreamt instead of Christmas in Big Sur and was in love with the Californian sunshine as I laboured through weapon theory and admired the IBM public relations approach. I didn't get to California till more than 30 years later after I'd first set eyes on the IBM data reality ad hanging up on the International Relations lecturer's wall. This CIA plant crapped on about thinking the unthinkable and the USA's imperialist role since 1945. I disliked the guy's mechanical voice which described crazed pictures of second-strike capacity and images of war games gone wrong.

"When you do a thesis you've got to think of yourself putting your imagination to work painting a cubist picture," he rasped.

This was hardly creative work in my view but I was stuck with the American Way that had infiltrated Scotland more or less completely, especially with the oil explorations in the North Sea. Dynamic conformity brought the lure of Madison Avenue to the land of porridge with the mirage of a liberal presence inside the military-industrial-complex. My synthetic US- directed internationalism was indebted to American publishers and Hollywood. At the Sociology Department I acted out the charade of freedom sincerely believing at the time that I was doing something different. I was full of ideas on mental illness, deviance and the alternative society where the commune movement held sway. I regurgitated the names of the moment reducing myself to the role of a word salad merchant who had lost his cool. My approach to everything was arrogant and silly as I assumed that I should be recognized as an infallible authority gifted with second sight. This was a mistake.

"I know where it's at, " I said foolishly as I embarked on a special goodbye trip all of my own construction. I failed to respond to criticism and suggested that intelligence shouldn't be measured in terms of ability to manage mass madness. I was unable to see that the only result of my frenetic studies was a boorish training in bureaucratic twaddle.

By the time I had got to the "varsity" the rules had tightened up. Gone were the great days when students got stoned in tutorials. As usual I had arrived too late. Instead of taking it easy I overdosed on a diet of meaninglessness and reacted in a paranoid fashion to any papers that were critical of the hippy movement. The radical literature as shown by Kenneth Keniston said that "we're all hippies now" but surely serious students of society had to dispense with such unrealistic dreams. I wanted to stop the future of disenchantment but didn't know that my naïve idealism was tied up with unsound delusions of grandeur. Of course I was as self-interested as anybody else in a world where the community had collapsed. Being alive in such a wasteland was a tragedy whatever the journals said in their convoluted pages so any experience was unlikely to produce any lasting solution. The absence of group awareness in the sick sphere of modern society made sure that "getting heads together" produced nothing more than good pop songs. The academic trip was starting to lose its shine as I scoffed at the choreography of the departmental show. I concluded that there weren't any subjects left in the mind-numbing finishing school.

I was being finished off. Kill them all shrieked Emperor Boukassa in a rage. I envisaged various riffraff disintegrating in a final assault on the knowledge base. I watched patrilineal systems dissolving along with micro-interactionism, structural – functionalism, Mertonians, Parsonians, anarcho-syndicalists and the "committed" Marxists who were only neurotic ex-Methodists in the vast academic zoo. My basic nihilism ensured that I would not progress as an academic. The endless communication game had worn me out. I wrote what I considered to be an inspired work of genius for Andy Rigby, a lecturer from Bradford. Rigby had seemed like a pal but he was just another system boy on the make. I had boiled with fury when he and his wife had cocked a snook at the waterfront slum on Waterloo Quay where I lived with my girlfriend. My fury was the same energy that fuelled my essay on "Obsolete Youth", an exercise in heavy-duty rejection of everything.

After more than 30 years, the contents seem to be holding up reasonably well in my opinion.

"One interpretation of youthful cynicism is as good as another. Cynicism hides unknown fears. Modern cynicism has metamorphosed into a cultist lapse. It is an easy option to go for Divine Light, Scientology, Process or the Unification Church. (Cults were once a topic of controversial interest) One year it is Che Guevara, the next John Lennon and the one after that there is a plastic re-incarnation of the King of the Jews. In the western tradition of the hero-worship charade so-called obsolete youth continues with a search for ever-elusive truth. Charisma remains in charge with fashion a close second...."

I pulled out my big guns as the bilge poured forth.

"...the true members of the sociological generation are those endowed with the sociological imagination. They are the truly obsolete. Obsolete are those who feel no interest in dynamic conformity, no enthusiasm for the fun life of the military industrial complex. The artist as the brother of the criminal and the madman has nothing to say to the experts at Headquarters. There are therefore two strategies useful in avoiding the internalisation of the norms of the dominant social system – total withdrawal or playing the system. The second strategy is the most common with the character of the "right guy" who surfaces more frequently in the social milieu of the USA and Western Europe. Although retreatism has milder forms of objection to pulling out completely it is the extreme versions with attract attention. Political life is unscrupulous without concern for morality. There are distinct ingredients for catastrophe – education, affluence, and free use of drugs of all kinds, racial discrimination and technology. Obsolete youth and the unwanted deviants cannot compromise where there is no room for compromise. The ethic of expediency is the order of the day...."

The message got wilder by the line.

"A problem previously considered to be minimal is blown up to epidemic proportions by an official moral crusade. Official paranoia feeds off such efforts and supports the consensus myth of the moral majority.

Attitudes will harden against deviant minorities due to pressure from central values. New social movements illustrate psychic unrest, the growth of awareness among isolated individuals and groups of individuals, corruption by media leading to movement dissolution and disappearance underground. The technocracies are able to divert the forces of dissent into a multiple range of activities, all provided courtesy of Big Daddy. The important question is whether dissent will come from the revolutionaries of the future or if dissent will be seen as futile when the system can satisfy any whim from unusual sexual needs to a weekend out on magic mushrooms. The morally bankrupt society cannot allow itself to recognize that the chronologically young have intellectualised their identities. The advertisers have encouraged personality change through product consciousness. The acid dream died a sad death in the degeneracy of Haight Ashbury as a supposedly divinely-inspire movement rapidly turned into a TV pop cartoon."

My word salads were inspired.

"By travelling the path of Kropotkin, Dostoiyevsky, Nietzsche et al, the sterility of human interaction and the buffoonery of social gamesmanship disappears into the void. The lost ones attempt all that is quite impossible. Possessing only illusions, they have forgotten how to pray but there are no directives if there is no belief. Meanwhile there is nothing to be done save wait for the next idea, the next joke. The exercise in semantics continues, as yesterday's conspiracy theory becomes today's poetic fancy. Consistency atrophies as the laughter explodes over the spires of infinity. Ha ha! What a laugh! Fade away Soft Machine".

"God help us all," retorted Rigby. "There's a need for a long discussion on the nature of a sociological essay. How can you say such things without evidence?" he asked.

I felt like bashing in Rigby's face and pulling out his scruffy beard, hair by hair – however there was no point in spending the next twenty years in Broadmoor, I reasoned. From that moment on Rigby and I were firm enemies and shortly afterwards I wrote the bastard a malevolent letter that was calculated to insult every fibre of his being.

"You are just another salaried pen-pusher who hopes to publish more worthless papers " I accused Rigby. "You live out in the country along with other proletarian expatriates trying to put on a show of getting back to the land by grazing a few sheep" I jeered. "The greening of academia is most unconvincing with fools like you about. Your outlook is as sick as the rotten silage you used for growing your mouldy potatoes. Take it from me, Mr.Utopia, that I'm happy to rubbish your wellies world of university trendies that pretend to be part of the soil."

Rigby fizzled with anger in his fair to middling way before eventually making his way back to where he belonged in redbrick territory. I sighed as yet another possibility of rapport crashed on take-off. Human relations were predictably disappointing. It was a shame that I wouldn't be joining the staff club or taking up the PhD sponsored by a Dutch university to study cargo cults in Polynesia. Despite everything I scraped through and got a degree although the general consensus was that I hadn't got the message with my "fuck you " attitude. I'd hardly been able to see beyond my student uniform of donkey jacket, jeans and polo neck. I'd given no attention to progressive issues like feminism, racism, gay rights and so on. I obviously wasn't interested in a fairer or more egalitarian society. I had the words but no convictions. Going to university was just my attempt to show that I had a brain. Now though I was confirmed in the unemployment stakes as yet another sociologist. I now had to rejoin the world.

.......................................................................................

# BACK IN THE WORLD

Trouble started almost immediately in the form of the Graduate Tutor.

"Welcome to Porton where we have an ethos of participation. We encourage discussion between students and tutors." The comprehensive school product gave out the usual phoney government line as my spirits sank into the dust. I saw nothing to discuss with the tutors who appeared as a dull, unhappy bunch who thought they were something special like me. I despised these old sports jackets on sight while there were few students to whom I could even begin to relate. Louise seemed OK at first but there was something bizarre about her hard-drinking habits and camp style. She shook her long hair as she held a Park Drive in her painted fingernails. Her conversation was insane.

" I know what a man wants, " she said. "Come back to my place"

"Well I'm not sure".

"Look I'll let you into a secret. I've actually had a sex change. I used to be a man".

I exited fast. The only other prospect was Fat Pat but I didn't fancy her at all. I was condemned to a lonely year. Time crawled by in the stifling world of teacher training. Students were obliged to keep a teaching file as a record of every second of ghastly encounters with the dregs of society in classrooms scattered round the parochial landscape. At Fleetwood secondary school children shouted abuse at the maddy from Scotland.

"Go back to Glasgow, Jimmy" they yelled.

Committed teachers commented disapprovingly on my shambolic classroom management.

"You've got to keep discipline".

"Well it's a downmarket scene. It's not my problem since I'm doing your job unpaid."

So much for the aims and objectives of the lesson.

I disliked the French tutor, a baldy goon who saw himself as the reincarnation of Jean-Paul Sartre even if he couldn't speak French. His attitude towards me was one of contempt so I decided to put the low fellow in his place.

"This is my lesson, Frenchy so I'd appreciate a civil good morning when you come into my classroom."

"You're only a student"

"And you're only a tutor who can't speak French."

"Get out of my office!"

I thought of taking a swing at the bastard but held back. I was learning to control my aggression.

"Once you have agreed to say good morning and treat me with a proper measure of respect then I'll leave," I said in my most reasonable tones. Compromise was the name of the game. The guy turned purple with rage but as there were witnesses present he had to comply with my request. After that he seemed to wise up. The Graduate Tutor though was a continuing problem.

"Now here's a clear example of the Tolpuddle Martyrs and their social origins," he said in his bright Lancastrian accent. He was giving a perfect lesson with slides, charts, maps and other gobbledygook scattered all over the tutorial room.

I asked him why anybody should be interested in the proletariat as shocked faces turned towards me.

"Your attitude is quite unacceptable, " he spluttered.

"So is yours" I sneered unfairly.

Somehow I again managed to scrape through another exercise in self-mortification and humiliation. I realized that I was making a serious mistake in joining the so-called "teaching profession". I didn't appear to have many other choices though as the job for losers was the only viable prospect on offer.

At the school on the Bristol Channel I got my first job as a probationary teacher. The head was a greasy pseudo-philosopher who enjoyed his paternalistic style of rule over his ridiculous school. The place catered for yobs and clowns stuck in an old Labour Party movie. My time in the Remedial Department was the most unrewarding in living memory. If only I had known what it would be like as I answered the head's oily questions at the interview.

"Oh and you play the piano? Wonderful. We're looking for somebody to organize the school concert."

"Yes I'm very keen to make a contribution to the extra-mural activities of the school."

The job had begun one dark day in November with fog swirling round the portakabin windows and a deep depression in my heart. It was as if I was back with Mr.Paisley at the Glasgow High School.

"Fuck off you big pouf!" shouted a revolting girl as I came into the remedial classroom. Inwardly I was furious to have ended up in this position, which didn't change much over time. Old Pape, the Head of Remedial smirked at the amusing spectacle of the newest member of staff being subjected to trial by ordeal. He was only waiting for another five years until retirement. He passed the time by remembering the war and the money he used to make as an old doughnut salesman. He was a good guy but I didn't want to be there.

"Now children" I said feebly just as Squeaky Smith had attempted to quell the riots in his Maths classes. But the response was more abuse as days, weeks, months passed in torment. Why was I enduring this deadening experience in government conditioning? I did have a mortgage to pay and this was the only legal way of financing it. Was I indeed experiencing everything as ordered by Professor Barnett? It was a joyless existence hardly helped by my colleagues in the staff room. It was bursting with sad songs, which had failed to sell. The Welsh male voice choir seemed to rule but I wasn't Welsh. I was almost sick when the Head of the Religious Studies Department asked me a meaningful question about the relationship between Christianity and Existentialism. I didn't attach much importance to Weatherhead's Christ but at least knew that Sartre was right to decide that Hell was other people. The probationary year dragged on with daily riots the norm. The tutor group was a shambles as I always marked everybody present before opening my morning newspaper and ignoring the surrounding chaos. I was always burrowing in the pages of the Times Educational Supplement for another job. I couldn't be bothered with the register, that holy document so beloved by the authorities. It made little difference to me whether or not the kids were present. No doubt these poor kids would be taking advantage of the enterprise culture so who was I to question their entrepreneurialism?

"Bryson"

"Present " said his friend Jones.

"Plummer".

"OK present."

My unpopularity with the other staff was legion as it became clear when I eventually resigned. From my own point of view I'd done my best, even giving morning assembly a shot. The Head was of the opinion that the school day should begin with an act of collective worship with a meaningful theme. When it came to my turn to address the throng I put on a reggae record and then "Beginning to see the light" by Andy Warhol and the Velvet Underground. But nothing I could do went down well with the Welsh choirmen and their supporters from a bygone age. So my contribution to the work of the school was reduced to a £1 book token plus a stupid card showing a stereotyped Scot lifting a scarlet kilt above a pair of grossly knobbly knees.

"Now Mr.Dullerson's always been a reading man," joked the Head at the boring presentation ceremony.

"Good luck Mr.Mr.Dullerson," he said as he handed over the bit of waste paper on which was written "Och aye but we never did see his knees."

I walked out without a backward glance throwing the scraps into the basket, relegating the names of the nobodies who had signed it to memory. It was another goodbye scene. I drove back up the motorway taking with me the tattered copy of the probation report that had been drawn up by the Head with extreme prejudice. I actually had to ask to see his comments and then laboriously write down in longhand as he refused to get me copy. Anyway how many people would survive in such an impossible situation?

I found having to control any class quite exhausting so I didn't waste any energy in a futile exercise. It was endless farce as far as I was concerned. One day an Inspector called to assess my incompetence. With 3D things were off the wall. I used to laugh and joke with the kids as they were completely switched off hearing about the reasons behind the Second World War. I should have said that I supported the Germans although there was no point in appearing so unpatriotic. Suddenly Mr.Plonkton from County Hall was putting me on the spot. I found myself having to talk nonsense about the Battle of the Atlantic and the convoy system.

"Now Churchill was keen with Roosevelt's support to give a massive boost to the Allied war effort..."

"Sir what are you talking about?"

"...The U boat campaign had been spectacularly successful in sinking the thousands of tons of Allied shipping and so threatened Britain with starvation..."

"Drop the act, sir. Look at these porn cards instead".

"Now 3D we'll be going through to see the Hitler film."

"Aww, sir we've seen it five times before."

Shouting kids ran out of the classroom knocking over chairs and desks.

"Mr.Dullerson! You are not in control!" Mr.Plonkton was beside himself.

"Yes I am."

"Can I see your lesson notes?"

I fumbled through a messy pile of scrap paper but couldn't find anything.

"I must have left them in the staff room."

Plonkton then ignored me as he took over the class and ordered the kids to sit down to watch the Hitler film for the sixth time. Meekly children did as they were told as old footage came on of the chocolate addict with the funny moustache. At the end of the lesson Mr.Plonkton put on his most serious expression.

"You didn't prepare this lesson, Mr.Dullerson."

"Yeh I did. Now it's Friday afternoon and I've got my weekend lined up. Excuse me."

"Mr.Dullerson!"

"Yeh see you,"

It was the same wherever I turned. In the Head's probation report I read about myself with detached interest.

"...clearly a highly intelligent young man but he does not appear to attach much importance to record keeping, arrives at School when the bell is ringing and leaves immediately when bell rings at the end of the day..." Right on I thought

".... children find his accent difficult to understand(!) and have difficulty in following his line of thought..." The report warbled on meaninglessly. I saw no reason why I should adjust my intellect to suit the empty demands of a bunch of slow learners.

"therefore in the circumstances I feel that it is necessary for Mr.Dullerson to have his probationary period extended by a further six months."

Later I tried to have this unjust decision revoked but the faceless bureaucrats at the DES in Darlington wouldn't hear of it. They were right as usual.

"The Department in perfectly satisfied that the Head followed procedures to the letter and that the assessment of Mr.Dullerson is fair and accurate. Therefore in accordance with the Report, he should have his probationary period extended by another six months when his teaching status can be reviewed." It all sounded rather ominous but thankfully there was no further inspection and to all intents and purposes I was a fully qualified teacher.

..........................................................................................

# IS THERE ANY SUPPLY WORK?

I could now earn lousy money and starve during the holidays as a supply teacher. The County had ample supply work for dropouts who found modern society an insult to the senses. The disaster of my education and the personal problems I'd had at home had led me up the garden path, a path choked with weeds of the most malignant variety. Looking further ahead all that could be seen were years of alienation and punishment with no hope of reprieve.

At the interview at the special school I gazed at the Head of Education, a party man. I saw the six different coloured telephones sitting on his desk and felt sorry for the unfortunate young ladies who had been incarcerated under the draconian Care Order acts. I didn't feel much in common with his beefy personality.

"I'm Bert Crandle, Head of Education and responsible for Philosophy. And this is Mr.Lee Merrick, our Senior Teacher with whom you'll be working."

Mr.Merrick had a long operation scar on his forehead that fronted his bald, pink skull. A voice came out speaking in a broad Yorkshire accent.

"Pleased to meet you Mr.Dullerson" said the Northern psycho.

"Delighted".

As the assistant senior teacher I was responsible for "behaviour modification" and the welfare of around twenty girls. Most of them had been sexually abused and there were several prostitutes among them. From the beginning I found the whole situation very upsetting. It was a daunting task getting the message across that I wasn't there to make life worse for the girls but rather that I wanted to help them. This wasn't easy when the main topic of conversation was sex, drugs and rock n' roll. Their language was quite unprintable along with their provocative behaviour. But as anybody who has worked in such a place, prison or psychiatric hospital you get used to anything.

"Now girls today it's project work – a pretext for painting activity with more discussion on the hopeless problems that plagued the unwilling inmates. The morning assembly began the day in an atmosphere of resentment with the management lined up on stage. I performed a macho act, which made me popular with the girls and unpopular with Crandle and his Home Office associates.

"Morning girls."

"Darling we love you" came the shouts.

They loved me because I couldn't bring myself to be the harsh, authoritarian figure desired by the hierarchy.

"I can't communicate with Dullerson," Merrick said in exasperation, his face crumpled up like the steel industry in Middlesborough. I couldn't communicate with him either so it was better to listen to the girls ripping into the "care staff" who were either mad or confirmed lackeys of the System.

"Mrs.Hayden, you're a screw," jeered Linda as Mrs.Hayden was reminded of her wasted years in the Prison Service. Various nasty characters wandered about the grounds of the school with large bunches of keys. There was a lock-up section where recalcitrant inmates were shut away. Fay looked like the young Mia Farrow and was all of 14. She had escaped but had been recaptured.

"This is your home, girls", Crandle preached. But Fay's cell didn't look like domestic bliss. The walls were covered with graffiti showing how much previous inhabitants had enjoyed life with the local authority.

"Fucking bastards. I want my Mom!"

"Rastaman pay the bail to stay out of jail".

"Crandle is a shite."

"Let me out of here, Mr.Dullerson" pleaded Fay.

"I'd love to " I said handing her a packet of forbidden cigarettes. "But I can't"

Her eyes looked up imploringly. What had she done to deserve being slammed up alone for days at a time? Her only visitors were people like Uncle Crandle, Merrick and myself. I had only escaped Fay's fate because of my "good background". A few weeks later on a school outing Fay did another runner. No doubt she would be picked up again and would be back inside. Such an angel should have had a better deal in life.

"We can't communicate with you..."

"I've already written my resignation, " I said indifferently as I threw down a crumpled statement at Crandle and his chums.

On the last morning at the assembly I announced that I was leaving. The girls cried and so did I but there was nothing I could do in such circumstances save walk away.

These were indeed wasted years with my career in tatters. I seemed to lack insight into the necessity of earning a living with the only option being supply teaching. And there was plenty of that – Merrywood Boys, Withywood, Bower Ashton, Hartcliffe Yate etc etc and special units such as the Stage Five Centre or Pucklechurch. All of them were terrible, fighting a losing battle against the overwhelming odds of social mayhem and disturbance. Crowds of louts shouted at the sincere woman trying to teach Maths at Withywood.

"Did you get it last night, Miss?"

"Show us a leg, darling"

The horrible headmistress came into the staff room where I was comfortably seated reading the "Guardian".

"There's been a bit of trouble down in the Maths Department. We'd like you to relieve Ms.Blythe who's been taken ill.

"Now you lot, settle down" I asserted my feeble authority as Ms.Blythe rushed out in floods of tears. An appalling hour lay ahead packed with quadratic equations and the bore of all things algebraic. I'd managed to get this job by putting forwards my Maths credentials. The Head of Maths, a bitter, twisted woman of 35 hadn't liked me from the first day.

"Now we expect all members of the Department to attend staff meetings," she announced crisply.

I looked at the shambles in the Maths Department and the grey, crushed faces of my colleagues. Why was this happening to me? I decided that I wouldn't be attending any meetings. Upstairs I struggled heroically to keep order with a group of savage thirteen year olds. Contrary to popular myths, teaching uppity kids is an impossible job unless you are thick-skinned and have that undefined teaching personality that delights in guiding young unformed minds. I wasn't like that. I expected kids to do what they were told and get on with their work, just as my own teachers did.

"Look sir, I've taken my trousers off," shrieked crazy Bob as the girls shouted with delight. Other boys ran about the classroom winding up the class to a fever pitch. I lost my temper as anybody would but it was different to when I had been at school. The teacher was powerless to do anything and losing control was regarded as a clear sign of weakness. Moments later I was called down to the Head's office to be told that the management were unhappy with my teaching.

"We've had reports about what's been happening in your classes."

"Really Miss Blenheim. I felt that things were going pretty well. In fact I was just saying to the Head of Department how interested the children were in quadratic equations."

"Look you have to leave the school NOW. Clearly you are quite unsuited to the profession and if you had been employed full-time then there would have certainly been an Enquiry."

Schools seemed much the same wherever you went. At Merrywood Boys. a large school stuck out on a Bristol post-war housing estate, it felt like 1957. The buzzer for classes sounded.

"Good morning schooolll" droned a sugary Birmingham voice over the tannoy.

"This is Mr.Price, the Deputy Headmaster. Fistfights must not take place in Trym House common room. This is an instruction from the Head of Trym House, Mr.Trym who is very prim. Also boys must congregate at the front of the building after school. On a more cheerful note, I would like to congratulate boys from Armstrong House who have won an away match with Withywood School 2:1 Well done, Armstrong boys. Reports will be issued this week by teachers in their tutor groups. I would like to remind boys and staff that this aspect of the work of the schooolll is very important. Mr,Scattlebury will be sending you all a reminder in a few days time. That is the end of today's announcements." With my colleague Mr.Reslet I appreciated the absurdity of all this and immediately began to mimic the treacly voice that had now retreated down the throat of the Deputy Head. Mr.Price was probably now stuck in his office with Joan, his ugly secretary. Mr.Reslet continued to be employed as a supply teacher at Merrywood mainly because he had caught Mr.Price in a most compromising position with Joan. Rather than have the office affair broadcast to the world, Mr.Price, with his sweaty bri-nylon shirt and gnomish expression, handed out the supply work as reward for keeping mum. The phone would go at 8 a.m. waking Mr.Reslet out of his stupor.

"Price here, would you be able to do what you usually do? A day's supply? You could? Right. See you then. Cheeriebye.

On a bad day the roles would be reversed with Mr.Reslet making the call to ask if there was any work available.

The standard question: "Is there any supply work?"

"Could I speak to Mr.Price, please?" as Joan answered at the school.

"Mr.Price here. Nice to hear from you, Mr.Reslet. Negative news I'm afraid. But we do have your details here and we'll be in touch soon."

For a while Mr.Reslet and I stayed in favour with the Merrywood hierarchy. You never knew when your status of flavour of the month would be replaced by a black mark against your name. You had to stay on your toes through the long and pointless hours. At Merrywood petty morality had free reign, Various school dignitaries kept a watchful eye on the possible subversion of educational dogma while nasty community policemen smiled quietly in a corner of the staff room. The "Police as a moral force" was much in evidence, an insidious development designed to crush all opposition. But I found it hard to take the whole situation seriously, thus falling out of favour with the powers that be. It was easy to get into trouble. Mr.Miles had called me in for a dressing-down after I'd read some explicit material to a class. A boy had wanted some interpretation from some harmless bit of steamy writing and I was happy to oblige.

"We do have our own biology teachers for furthering the cause of knowledge in this delicate area". Miles murmured unpleasantly as I turned away in fake remorse. It seemed ridiculous to present the view that sex had no social context. Was literary criticism going to become illegal too I asked Mr.Miles. Mr.Reslet too had landed in hot water after Mr.Price had ordered him to "take a more active supervision of classes." In other words, he had to stay awake, difficult for him after yet another night out clubbing. You had to keep your eye on the ball, otherwise you would fall victim to the lynx-eyed thought police, inspectors, appraisers and other time and motion robots whose job was to make a teacher's life as hard as possible. The new managerialism made sure that staff monitoring played an important role in the educational process. In other words nobody was a free agent with schools becoming hotbeds of gossip, unfounded allegations and character assassination. Hypocrisy and dishonesty ruled the pedagogical obstacle race and so guaranteeing that original or innovative teaching was ground into clouds of chalk dust. Teachers against their better judgement found themselves to be unwilling participants in an endless game of institutional conditioning. Monitors in the classroom might have disappeared long ago but there were eyes and ears everywhere. It seemed so unfair as teachers were being made responsible for the society that encouraged children to do what their TV told them. In a world of unmanageable contradictions teachers were seen as irrelevant authority figures, fair game for anybody. It was only too easy to blot your copybook.

Mr.Reslet had come up against it after complaints had come in about his experimental drama classes. Colleagues had been outraged by unheard-of classroom scenes. The drama queen's lessons were little more than mayhem as kids let it all hang out to the sound of raucous disco music.

"Never in thirty years of teaching have I been witness to such a scandal" roared the Head at the Devon school, after making adverse comments on Mr.Reslet's fitness for the profession. "Oh we had such hopes when you first came to us. But you've let us down badly I'm afraid. You're not popular at all. You should never have joined the profession and if you hadn't resigned then moves would have been taken to affect your removal. I've had concerned parents (always a red rag to a bull) phoning in while there have been constant rumours about your indifference to good discipline. I can't recommend you for a permanent position after your dismal performance here."

So the odds were stacked against anybody who was still a human being. As far as I was concerned disapproval followed me around like a bad smell. The Bristol scene went absolutely nowhere and there was no promotion. The years vanished in a sea of shouting, stuffy school dining halls, hostile staff rooms, pained expressions and a particularly empty bank account. Teaching at this level was an exercise in total defeat with me denying my essence in the lost cause of understanding the needs and problems of a wholly indifferent clientele. No doubt the scenario was being repeated in schools throughout the land although it took more time for me to realize that I wasn't the only one who considered that "education" had little or nothing to do with the brutality of real life. There was no end to the way. The nonsense continued from Blackpool to Brent, one of the "loony boroughs" from North London.

"Teachers!!" screeched the headline in the C2 tabloid. "I used to respect teachers. They used to know what to do. I've bettered myself with my own building business but what about those teachers? A bunch of scruffs who don't know what a day's work is about. All they do now is to preach about social rights when they should be teaching ". It was the 1987 loadsamoney period as the low taste ragsheets raved on. Building businesses were sprouting up with the latest property boom so it was no wonder that builders were losing themselves in delusions of grandeur, imagining that they were going to join the gentry in their green wellies. They must have forgotten they lived in the U.K.

"Teachers!" said the sour female Anna. , also a teacher in fact. "They live in an unreal world. I've been in the real world where you have to work. I had my own advertising agency employing my own staff. Now I owe the bank and can't pay my mortgage." She scowled self-importantly, another unwilling teacher who as a business bigot would never understand anybody else's point of view.

" So if you were so successful what are you doing here on supply? " I asked politely.

"These people think that the world owes them a living". Anna made an irrelevant comment.

I felt bound to defend the noble calling. "These people as you patronisingly describe them have all sorts of reasons for being teachers. If you despise them so much why don't you go back to Saatchi and Saatchi or whatever they're called?"

"Don't you dare tell me what to do!" she retorted.

"Look, I'm having my dinner. I don't need to be bothered and anyway I've got bills to pay too," I spat back

At trendy Holland Park School the supply teachers sat about in the staff room waiting for the call to duty. At least back in the early 90s you got paid properly, £500 every week and a good dinner every day down at Kensington and Chelsea's administration building. Compare that situation with now when I'm nowhere near this figure.

You can put up with a fair amount of psychological torture at £100 per day in 1990 and there was always the park at the back of the school to enjoy after you'd left the sounds of derangement behind. Al Qaeda hadn't yet appeared but the Islamic thing could be a problem.

"Kill Rushdie!" yelled a group of Moroccan boys.

"Look this is still a democracy. Rushdie can say what he likes in his books. Religion in this culture is a personal matter."

"You insult our God teacher."

"Rubbish. I'm insulting nothing. You can believe what you want. By the way have you ever read the Satanic Verses?"

SILENCE.

Later on that day.

"Now we've had complaints that you've been making racist remarks." The right-on Deputy Head Jane Shallice wore an expression of disapproving socialist fundamentalism.

"I've been doing nothing of the sort."

"Well Mohammed Al-Tourbi feels that you were casting negative aspersions on his religion."

"You mean that's how you want to interpret the situation, Deputy Head."

"That will be all, Mr.Dullerson. Please remember the cultural sensitivities of our children " she lectured.

"Bitch" I muttered as I went out to face more moronic mobs.

"You got personal problems sir. You on drugs, sir?" Insolent characters with baseball caps sneered at me in this school where there seemed to be no discipline at all. I could only splutter in rage and attempt to show that I was in command. Some hope in cosmopolitan London. I found it hard to identify with the sincere belief among the staff that they would win their rearguard action for the now defunct London Education Authority. The Conservatives were making sure that it was all over with the Labour Party dream and the local management of schools initiative was close at hand, putting supplies out of a job. Life was great at the bottom. At leafy Holland Park the failure of the comprehensive system was made plain. Anthony Wedgewood Benn was lisping nonsensically at a staff meeting on the "imperialist attack on Iraq. Blinkered ditherers and clowns talked rubbish about the unspeakable Ba'ath murderers.

"When I was talking with Shaddam Hushain in Baghdad the other day there was Edward Heath" garbled Benn. Yes Tony. Here I was lost among the liberals but I had to pretend to be one myself and had done so for years. It was the only way to survive in the world of Newspeak, Newsweek and News. We were all aspiring Vicars of Bray. I found it impossible to understand what the first trendy comprehensive was supposed to be on about. The old hippy Australian was more on the ball.

"The thing about Britain is that it just doesn't work properly" he commented.

"Like your race problem .You need to take things in hand like I did yesterday. Some of these big coons were playing up so I took a couple of them outside and dusted them up. When they complained to the management I was complimented on my firm approach. " The old beardy laughed cynically. I didn't necessarily agree with the Aussie but there was no doubt that the true nature of race relations in schools was hidden from the public gaze. I remember my friend Mr.Beg from Pakistan who always came in for racist remarks from West Indian yobs.

"Go back to Karachi Paki" they yelled. What could he do but remain in Wembley and keep working to make up his losses on the stockmarket? Mr.Beg was as British as anybody else and a good human being. What had he done to get abused by ignoramuses in shell suits? He just happened to be born in Pakistan while I had appeared in Scotland. Personally I thought that racial stereotyping was pretty silly but it was all over the place. I objected to the idea that the race war was the white man's entire fault as much as the view that all ethnic minorities were born victims.

I found plenty of schools where whites weren't highly regarded. Alperton High School was a good example of political correctness gone astray. This Brent school was celebrating Divali, no doubt because the Deputy Head was of the Hindu persuasion. Nobody had ever heard of Christmas in Brent except of course in the shops of Wembley High Street. White traitors sat about pretending to be of mixed race when they were mostly Irish. Crowds of mad and hopelessly alienated children shouted at me as I got out my old jalopy.

"He's a supply teacher you know. Hey white boy!"

I strode purposefully into the classroom, trying to quieten the awful din. I glanced at the newspaper lying on the desk.

"Put that paper away immediately and start work," screamed a sharp soprano voice that took me completely by surprise.

"Who was that?" I asked the class.

"That's Ms Cranthone the Acting Deputy Head. Oohh sir, you'll be getting the sack " jeered the wideboys.

"Now look, just shut up and get on with your work. Page 7 & 8. Do the section on the production system."

"Are you a proper teacher, sir? Are you married, sir? Are you gay, sir? Why did you become a teacher, sir?"

"Shut up for the twentieth time. If there's any more trouble I'll arrange a detention." I made the usual empty threats.

The class eventually settled down and pretended to work as I fired off a note to the mental Acting Deputy Head. She hadn't learnt her part properly in the last training seminar.

"Don't you dare interrupt my lesson. I've never met you before and I don't care who you are!" I wrote angrily on a scrap of paper.

After class the predictable surprise was waiting.

"Could you come down to the office, Mr.Dullerson?" A trusty was standing in the corridor. Down at the office the owner of the sharp soprano voice faced him from the seat of power.

"Well you can see who I am now, can't you" she said. The old dyke was dressed up in a mini-skirt but her expression was from the land of the separatists.

"OK I can appreciate your position but it was pretty disconcerting to be undermined like that. I'm not used to such a situation."

"I decide who works here. Do you want to come back tomorrow, Mr.Dullerson?"

I thought of my flat in negative equity and the ever-increasing overdraft with Barclays Bank.

"Yes of course. I really believe in all the good things you are doing here, Ms.Cranthone."

So I was back the next day and for years after that. A face was always needed to fill a space in front of other faces. I was a supply with attitude along with some other characters in the same boat.

"They're supplies you know" the other proper teachers remarked condescendingly.

At the great Alperton High School it was a Baker Day, which was taken up with a boring meeting. All training days were excruciatingly dull. Dr.Finkelstein from the Okabuku Institute in Kampala was delivering his Third World platitudes to his yawning audience.

"Charismatic teaching is the future according to tests carried out by Professor Said Abubakir at the Majnoon Training Center in Riyadh. " I imagined dark images of awful Pakistani military officers homing in on intimidated language instructors working for British Aerospace.

"This participle not gerund. You no charismatic, you no good Engleezi teacher. Empire over white boy."

At the back of the hall, rough PE types, white boys of course, smirked at the freak from Kampala. I continued to read my "Guardian".

"It's all fucking rubbish, know what I mean " scoffed Anthony Torrance, the ex-factory worker from Luton and Essex sociology graduate. The thing is that all these middle class women daren't say a word against a nigger like me and I know it. O'right darling? So I play the race card to the limit". Back in the staff room he lifted up the telephone to score. He was wonderful. He gave an added sparkle to everything.

I have fond memories of playing old Otis Redding numbers on the piano at Alperton.

I looked over at the politically correct Ms.Head who was now wondering what sort of characters she had welcomed to the "team". Brent was full of chancers and oddballs and I was one of them.

"OK white man you go and see the Subject Heads about the day's work".

I'd just walked into the staff room in Willesden High School. I t was 9.45 a.m. on any morning. Destroyed faces stared out of the institutional despair.

The Head was only too pleased to be putting me through my paces. He was black. I was white.

"You know white boy, there are a lot of social problems here" sneered Ernie the Head.

I thought this guy was a bigshit from Kingston but I didn't say anything since I was working for Brent, a hotspot of radical politics and corruption. I wanted to tell the black Mafioso to stuff race relations up his arse but I desisted. Downstairs the new French assistante from the Sorbonne was being massacred in the wrecked language lab. West Indian rude boys ridiculed her attempts to keep order. Ernie's Touton Macoute expression came round the door. This was the way you were welcomed to the end in London NW10. Ernie was enjoying the new version of apartheid.

Meanwhile outside the school gates the only slogan was "Loadsa-money we're the culture" It was 1987 but supply teachers like me weren't making a fortune. Instead we were waiting to be paid. Doors slammed. Fists bashed against bulletproof glass. Voices shouted in helpless anger.

"I've worked for ten weeks now and I haven't seen a salary cheque. I want my money. Give me my money!" Furious voices screamed at indifferent Indian clerks.

The scene was repeated day after day to no avail. Back in the staff room a letter in my pigeonhole spoke of a serious criminal offence.

"In response to complaints about your attitude at the pay office the other day, Mr.Dullerson, when you took it upon yourself to lecture my staff on the alleged deficiencies of the system, you are ordered to attend an inquiry at the Education Office."

I consulted with the NUT representative who was used to such letters. Brent was renowned for treating its employees like dirt. In due course I got up to the Education Office at the grim Wembley headquarters. The self-important female holding the post of Sexual Harassment Officer asked me why I had been "making comments" to a female member of staff. I vaguely remembered the sharp blonde in a mini-skirt.

"I was saying that I was unhappy with my pay situation" I said angrily. What was this Kafkaesque nightmare? It was Christmas the season of goodwill but not in Brent apparently. Contemptuously the Chief Education Officer wrote out a cheque. He saw himself as a professional Santa Claus.

"Here's £100, " he said. "Now you must post-date two cheques for that amount payable to the Education Department."

"But what about the rest of my salary?" I protested.

"It will come in due course through proper channels" was the unhelpful response from his dirty white duffel coat. I wondered about the keen and enthusiastic teachers of myth beloved by the Ministry of Education as I walked off into yet another poverty-stricken holiday. How could anybody be a committed teacher with this sort of thing going on? It could only be deluded fanatics who saw themselves as upwardly mobile in the uncritical world of the clueless society. I was going the opposite way and there seemed as though there was nothing I could do to getting closer to the street. Unlike Edith Piaf, teachers regretted everything. They were sorry about their misguided idealism, their naivety, and their failure to operate effectively in the "real world". I was one of them who had condemned myself to a life of subservience and mediocrity.

Going into a classroom is taking a step into your childhood. Maybe the teachers don't wear gowns any more but the chalk dust still lies everywhere covering the books, piles of pens, rubbers, paper and the other paraphernalia of institutional brain damage. You might see the odd pinstripe suit these days as part of the new management image while in one of the fundamentalist technology colleges you could come across some Rhodes Boyson type extolling some cheesy version of the Christian virtues. Generally though the individual teacher looks as he/she always did – a living picture of self-hatred and alienation. They're still in a permanent bad temper as you would be if you had to deal with armies of lunatics every day of the week, let alone spend every evening till midnight doing paperwork. Teachers look tatty with blotchy faces, pale from the endless pressure. They're not having fun.

"Students in 1969 were much more politically engaged as opposed to the present impasse."

The earnest teacher with his dandruff and Gerry Adams beard and spectacles dribbled over his cress sandwich in the History Department. The dandruff remembered the glorious days at Tadcaster College when they had done Morris dancing on the staff lawn.

"Oh yes these were the days. The Beatles, the Rolling Stones, Bernadine Dorn and the Weathermen, Allen Ginsberg, the love-ins at Berkeley."

The class yawned. Old Dandruff was one of yesterday's men. He'd never really developed beyond the hippy years. He adjusted his spectacles. Nobody had ever read his brilliant insights into the sex, drugs and rock n' roll bonanza. Publishers had thrown his stuff away unread. The class were on anti-depressants and didn't need any more of Old Dandruff's bipolar gloom. He droned on.

"Actually class I'm really open-minded. I was talking to the janitors the other day and was really interested in what they had to say.Yeah man. Staff rooms the same round the globe except in your head there's some notion of diversity. Don't need no education, don't need no mind control. Mock at the dirty fascism of political correctness and institutional feminism. It don't add up Jackson. Being a teacher I mean. Coming across as all proper and smart like they're just poofters. Know what I mean. Yo hate them all."

"Hopelessly dated" – Heinemann

"Not for our readers I'm afraid " – Times Educational Supplement"

"Quite unsuitable material for a serious publication like ours" – GTC newsletter

"You get nothing with a college diploma " – Frank Zappa

"Give us a break " Al Ahram

"Rubbish" – Home Office staff magazine, Broadmoor.

In the UK the state education system is a mess, whatever the politicians say. Government spokesman are always crapping on about improving standards of attainment when the reality is that standards are falling apart. Orwellian news management ensures that the true picture of the nation's schools is kept well under wraps. What is happening is not the fault of the teachers. The responsibility for the educational malaise is rooted in the celebrity fixation and the notion that money is the only standard of assessment. The system is still obsessed by examinations so the only point of school for the majority of children is having a social life and learning purely for good results. There is little interest in real learning as in any case the teacher is duty bound to follow a rigid syllabus. No deviation is allowed or else you're down at the Job Club learning how to write a CV for a job as a temporary lavatory attendant. Nihilism really seems to have won since ignorance is the new standard. Unpleasant government lackeys make the teacher's job almost unbearable with endless curriculum changes; new tests, new rules and regulations based on bigotry and antiquated paternalism. The general public view teachers as an odd bunch at best and a crowd of dangerous perverts at the other end of the spectrum. Various high profile cases have justifiably put teachers in a poor light even if the vast majority are model citizens. There is official paranoia over such taboo subjects such as sex and drugs, thus making nonsense of free expression. Only "specialists" are allowed to make pronouncements in these important areas while most teachers don't really want to rock the boat. They want to get their pensions and have lost their idealism aeons ago.

But I wasn't on the pension list. I was just a supply teacher, a despised breed who kept the whole shoddy edifice ticking along. I had trouble in Scotland with the General Teaching Council in Edinburgh. I'd got myself a good honours degree in Sociology, but due to the dominance of Psychology in educational thinking my degree wasn't considered appropriate for secondary teacher training. There seemed no justification whatsoever for this stance so I went to England where things were a bit more flexible. I spent years teaching a variety of subject including French, History and Government and Politics among others. Coming back to Scotland I was informed that I could be registered as a teacher with the GTC with the proviso that I should take further courses in French and Modern Studies to bring myself up to "the Scottish standard." Despite having been born in Scotland and educated at Glasgow High School and Aberdeen University, I felt as though I was being subjected to the in-built hostility to all things English that is an integral part of the self-important Scottish "culture". The general attitude to Sociology was one of total ignorance about its subject content and intellectual orientation. There was no logical reason for the deliberate policy of trying to prevent Sociology graduates from taking up secondary training in Scotland. No doubt because Sociology questioned the validity of psychological perspectives the educational status quo felt threatened by criticisms that were long overdue. It was if the GTC thought of a qualification in Sociology as being more like a certificate in Scientology or seminar training, a ridiculous comparison.

So I objected strongly to having European directives on qualifications blatantly disregarded by the peculiar subject-specific outlook of the Scottish Education Department. There was no finance available for the proposed upgrade and I wasn't in a position to waste a year studying for entirely un-necessary bits of paper. I'd covered all aspects of the English curriculum over the years and felt perfectly competent to teach French or anything else. I secured some supply work in the wilds of North East Scotland where I encountered viewpoints reminiscent of the "Prime of Miss Jean Brodie".

I was at Banff Academy covering Modern Studies, a mish mash of material that is very much like the English subject of Social Studies. I was working in conjunction with Mrs. McDonald, an uptight, disapproving character who didn't like anybody from outside the Banff and Buchan area. She must have thought I was English while she didn't take to my casual approach, hairstyle and unconventional attire.

"Did you do your training in Scotland?"

"No, I went to England because the system is much more flexible there. Anyway at Porton it was all continuous assessment which is much fairer, don't you think Mrs.McDonald?" She obviously thought that it was only the English who had anything to do with England and couldn't understand why I hadn't gone to Moray House in Edinburgh. In her opinion it was only lapsed members of the Church of Scotland who would even consider doing an inferior training among the Sassenachs. I could only agree, as I hadn't made it to full membership of Wellington Church.

Meanwhile my correspondence with the General Teaching Council in Edinburgh was getting nowhere at all. My reasoned arguments fell on deaf ears. Why should Sociology be regarded as an unsuitable subject for secondary training even when the GTC had awarded me a provisional teaching qualification in exactly that same subject? I was certainly allowed to teach in secondary schools but not specifically French or Modern Studies, subjects in which I was more than adequately qualified. I decided not bother attending the GTC meeting on my case as I would have probably lost my temper and damaged my lost cause even further. In the event I was recognized as being a qualified teacher able to teach the ("rarely taught") subject of Sociology.

My comment to the Times Educational Supplement on the saga was that the whole thing was absurd. The whole issue of what was a subject and what wasn't wouldn't disappear. Somewhere many subjects were interconnected - for instance there's little point in studying Physics unless your Maths is up to scratch. Nobody had pointed that out to me at school. What was all this stuff about subject specialism when often a more general approach was more than viable? Having studied Sociology I had already studied broadly. The debate seemed utterly puerile and petty-minded. A spokesperson for the GTC had said that all teachers had to be properly qualified and that the GTC couldn't put its hand up it if this wasn't the case. The bureaucratic stupidity of the situation was beyond words.

Whatever, I continued to labour as a supply. At Keith Grammar School somewhere north of Aberdeen the staff room was as Scottish as it gets. Stuffies sat about.

"You're not from these parts how is it in Holland?" came a comment from an old Jimmy smoking a pipe.

"Look I went to Aberdeen University, I was born in Glasgow and my grandmother came from Thurso. So I'm not Dutch as you imply and I'm as Scottish as you are even if I don't talk Doric" (the local dialect).

You couldn't win against parochial prejudice and bigotry.

"This is fucking rubbish ye ken," swore William McKenzie.

"Now look, Billy, don't swear in class."

"The name's William"

"Well Bill, open your jotter."

"I'm nae interested. You've got an old heap of a Volvo. Alvin Allan kens you oot at Berryhillock. He doesnae like ye."

"Now William, you've got to study French. It could always be useful."

"I'm nae doing it."

"Well just sit quietly and read a book."

Later the reports went in and like all reports the content had to be positive.

"William has improved in the social competence sphere this session and is making progress in his grasp of the subject."

The scowling Head of French instructed me to give the class an exercise in making Christmas cards - in French of course.

" Ask the class to write out in French as they listen to exercises on tape."

The classroom had tape recorders all round the room. I knew that the class weren't remotely concerned about the unknown festival of "Noel" and were using the tape recorders to listen to their own music. The end result was a disaster all round.

I handed the cards to the swine who informed me disapprovingly that the material was quite unsuitable.

"French j'aime Not. Noel no good. Francais crap." Etc

I looked at him. I had nothing further to say. It was all par for the course.

At Fraserburgh I lost control of a class of young savages. Things had been building up to a major confrontation.

"Yer nae frae they pairts" shouted the Fraserburgh fishermen. Awa back tae London ye English git" came the shouts of the choochter mobsters.

I was tired of driving 90 miles round trip to work every day and fed up with listening to insults. The way things are up in that part of the country Peterhead is a foreign land while Aberdeen is on another planet. In the Languages Department I wasn't popular with the strait-laced Head of Department who clearly found it impossible to relate to me. The lessons in madness continued till things came to a crunch. After yet another vain attempt to control a class of young hooligans I threw my books down on the desk and walked out of the school, never to return. Au revoir mes eleves. I was confirmed as a failed language specialist

Wherever you go you come up against the in-crowd. At the university pre-sessional in Aberdeen the attitude of the permanent members of the English Department was that outsiders were best ignored and preferably forgotten. I was returning to my Alma Mater as a Tefler. Dismal jimmies were everywhere.

"Coffee is only for members of the department," snapped the office secretary."

" Stay away from that shortbread " ordered the miserable caretaker".

" Now we want all temporary lecturers to make a proper input to the development of learning materials," the nasty young Ms pontificated to the oldsters.

Denis Regan and I just took the afternoon off instead. Why should we assist the workload of these lazy full-time people? We were being treated as worse than peasants.

"You must pay for your accommodation in advance," said the dour porter at the bleak halls of residence.

"We're very concerned that you are not teaching the required material," the supervisor said – a snide tactic to satisfy the curriculum police that all temporary lecturers were incompetent by definition. All these wind-ups had to be endured when we were only there for 4 weeks! I'd driven almost

800 miles up from the South of England. No travelling expenses were allowable. The mere privilege of teaching South Korean electrical engineers should have been more than enough compensation.

At the pre-sessional Overseas Graduate course at the frightful university of Birmingham I looked across at my students. The three Chinese among them looked expectantly at the Political Commissar.

"I am polymer nuclear physicist, " Mr.Chan said proudly.

Mr.Chan didn't know about my Physics marks at Glasgow High School. But I was the Science Co-ordinator. I was also a methodologist.

"Yes sir, there are thousands of universities in China and millions of nuclear specialists like me " continued Mr.Chan. He was being assessed for his presentation skills. The board was covered with incomprehensible technical drawing and unreadable equations and diagrams. He was trying his best and in English. I wondered how I would have done in Mandarin. I liked to encourage students.

"Uh, quite so, Mr.Chan. Full marks. Impressive work"

I took the lousy pay.

"You a teacher?" spat the earring boy.

"Yes."

"Need O levels?"

"Oh no."

"How much do you get paid then?"

"Oh £1 an hour."

The earring boy spat to prove it was infinitely better to be an earring boy.

"Ya git nufink with a college diploma, sir"

"Quite so."

"Right here's your supply sheet for the day" said the Deputy Head with the earring.

I looked at his carefully cultivated stubble and shaved head. He was a trendy teacher.

I wasn't. The sheet listed teachers by number- supply 1, supply 2, and supply 3. I felt totally depersonalised. The earring teacher didn't care at all. He was on a good whack.

The wasted years go by. The teaching years have made you old, messed up by pretending to be anybody but yourself. Look at the dandruff on your frayed collar, Mr.Jones. Seems as though you can't afford new cloth. What happened to all those bright ideals back at college in Merthyr Tydfil. Does anybody care about your browbeaten, neurotic expression and all the dried-up emotions that have been thrown away on millions of thickoes who worked down the market and thought teachers were nutters. Seems as though you have worn yourself out with heartache. It's all a mistake but it's too late to change now, Taffy. You're getting on and you can't take it the way you used to. I knew that feeling well. At the school in Bodmin it was a baking summer afternoon. French again.

"Fucking retard" came the insult from the back of the classroom. I raged at this character who staff later informed me was " a very difficult boy". I'd had quite a lot of work in the asylum town, most of it confrontational and problematic. I came into the "non-languages" French class. I looked up at the board where crude remarks were written about me.

"Mr.Dullerson is a turd. He stinks of old lavatories." A picture of a fresh turd graced the blackboard.

" Are you a muff diver?" asked a mad boy at the back. I refused to give a civil answer to his question.

Dealing with such commentary is stressful, particularly when kids can make remarks without much fear of any serious consequences. At Bodmin kids were encouraged to write out their account of an incident then apologise for their misbehaviour. The usual format was the request for " a fresh start" which in practice meant that miscreants could come back into the classroom and continue where they left off. The same situation is repeated everywhere. At the time you can be mortally offended by appalling behaviour and disrespect but incidents become blurred over time and are too numerous to mention. The problem has got out of hand with little being done to tackle indiscipline both inside and outside of school. Some schools are worse than others of course but the general direction is downwards. You can't even walk down the street without being accosted. I was in Truro one afternoon when I heard a shout of recognition.

"Hey teacher!" I felt like a Jew in Germany.

My usual response in such a situation is to make a half-hearted acknowledgement rather than show great friendliness. The alternative is to entirely ignore such a greeting.

"Oh hello " I said half-heartedly to a crowd of nasty-looking teenagers.

Next thing I knew was a cry of "fuck you" as the boy vanished down the crowded street. I was determined to follow this up and fortunately a few weeks later I was able to nail him at the tough school in St.Austell. "He should be gassed in any normal society" was the laconic response from cynics sitting round the science area.

Another time I was walking home with my shopping, a normal thing to do. I looked up at three or four feral-looking youths sitting on a park bench.

"Hey you teacher. You teach at our school? one of them shouted out.

"Yes". I'd been slaughtered in their school on many occasions and had no intention of going back there if I could avoid the place. There was little discipline since the management practiced a divide and rule policy. Children were always right and staff were always wrong. According to the irresponsible management, if a lesson went wrong then this was the teacher's fault for not making lessons interesting. Failure to inspire a totally uninspiring clientele was regarded as personal inadequacy. Rather than take effective measures to deal with insolence, rudeness and downright hostility the management preferred to do nothing. They could afford to on their large salaries.

"Hey teacher, take off those stupid dark glasses!"

I walked away in disgust, feeling vulnerable and alone.

"Fuck off!" said one of the nasty youths.

"Mind your manners!" I responded feebly, unwilling to get into a public confrontation. There was nothing I could do save walk away. Any attempt to get their names would have failed and besides I was only a supply teacher, an old punch bag in their jaundiced view. I took a deep breath and went home in a fury, knowing that I was reaching my limits when dealing with anti-social teenage behaviour. It was no use saying that I had been a teenager once – I was no longer a teenager but a middle-aged man with a middle-aged outlook. It was time to go but go where? At the present juncture the supply teacher is under siege with moves to replace the hapless bit part with full-time supply cover assistants. It's all in the name of cost-effectiveness. So what if nationally negotiated salary agreements are blatantly undermined and unqualified staff are put in? The unions don't seem to have much influence over developments and are mainly concerned with the interests of full-timers. It might not be a great job at piss poor rates of pay but the supply teacher fulfils an essential need. Also, at my age it's impossible to get another line of work if you're over 55 like me. I may be a piano player like Clint Eastwood but nobody's going to give me a slot in their nightclub. I'm not famous and am completely unknown, lost in eternal obscurity.

Most teachers can't take the daily stress so have to take days off to recover from the endless grind. That's the where the supply comes in – saving the nation from the school system collapsing in disorder and mayhem. Would you like to do the supply teacher's thankless task?

There's little support for the teacher in the classroom. Teachers have to listen instead to sanctimonious sermons about failing teachers and failing schools. Nobody seems capable of standing up to the government bullies who are motivated only by bureaucratic self-interest. For myself I'm not really interested in having a "proper job" in a comprehensive school. I have no wish to put up with the insidious testing regime that is just another problem in addition to rowdy classes, a mistaken emphasis on academic attainment and the unwanted intrusion of snooping time and motion lackeys. You can only mock the meaningless platitudes of "education, education, education" in the face of a directed denigration of professional expertise. A new educational McCarthyism is alive and well. Nevertheless you persevere in the face of unavoidable adversity. No doubt I should relax and take it easy but I can't and won't.

Schools are hiding a host of social problems that are set to explode at some stage. Just wait for the fireworks and don't blame the teachers.

Today I'm at the "sports college" doing music. It is fashionable now to call schools "colleges" and pupils " students" when they are still schools and pupils. As the mad music lessons progress I've got plenty of time to consider what's wrong with the world.

"Now fill in these worksheets carefully. Take a ruler and pencil so that you can draw the keyboard, then put in the names of the notes. A, B. C. D, E, F, G and so on. Remember there is no "H".

The class grumbled at yet another supply lesson and more pointless worksheets. You could say that music lessons were "challenging" if such a description covers the awful confrontations and unbearable noise. If you've spent time away from the chalkface what impresses you most is the noise. Music lessons were notoriously hard. All the kids ever wanted to do was listen to their kind of music. It would have been more appropriate to have a classroom disco than attempt to show the kids the difference between major and minor chords. I wished I was deaf as the noise reached crescendo pitch. I hadn't shouted at anybody for 6 years or more till I was back in the classroom again. That's what is so exhausting, the need to shout down the opposition who are using every trick in the book to make you crack. I shouted on, dealing with psychos from the bottom of society. I found the level of hostility and aggression quite astonishing even if I understood perfectly well that some children had the most dreadful lives at home. You heard tales of parents in prison, domestic violence and criminal outlooks as the norm. I couldn't do anything about any of that, as I wasn't a social worker. I did sympathise with the wretched of the Earth but all I could do, as a paper musician was shout. Shouting was essential for your very survival as the softly softly approach didn't have any effect whatsoever. I shouted at a young thug who climbed all over desks before opening the classroom window and running off. Doubtless he would be in jail a few years down the line. I nursed my sore throat.

"I'm outta here " I imagined but I wasn't. I needed the money to pay the Bank.

Class after class laid into me. I felt like an old man incapable of handling impossible children in a world gone completely off the rails. After school it always took hours to recover from the daily punishment detail.

It was Bodmin yet again. "Bonjour mes eleves. Draw pictures of places where you live. Write down the vocabulary in French and English." There was an indifferent response from the class. Michael Sharp ran out of the room saying that he had "mental problems" and needed to get his pills from the office. I could only agree with him. There were no pencils I discover and they have to be obtained from M.Pirot's room down the corridor. I am bombarded with repeated requests to leave the room.

"Sir, I'm bursting. Sir I have to go to the office to see my mother who is bringing in my drama poem at noon." All the kids know fine that they are not allowed out the room during a lesson but that's the way things go. The lesson stumbles on. I reflect on the dreadful lessons I put up with in this same school more than two years before. Suddenly my depressing reveries were interrupted by a senior management heavy who came into the room just as pencils were being thrown all over the place. There was a stunned silence in the presence of proper authority. Nobody listens to a supply but they stand to attention when bosses are present. Once the boss guy leaves things get back to the usual chaos. The next lesson was equally crazy – a low level English group who were asked to read a simple story and answer questions. Appallingly behaved boys showed off in yet another episode of indiscipline and farce. At the end of this I retreated to the staff room where of course nobody talks to me. I am a supply teacher after all and not a fully participating member of staff. I thank my lucky stars for the wise decision I made all those years ago – never to be a full-time teacher in a British state school. I don't want to die on the job.

In room 40 boys sit jeering at the back. It's another worksheet lesson. Gareth Williams and Peter Megarry sit doing nothing in keeping with their boorish and imbecilic attitude. My stomach rumbles in protest after the spicy meal from last night and having to put up with more Muzak mayhem. Eventually the class degenerates into anarchy as a group of thugs persecuted a fat boy for being fat. I saw him being baited like a dancing bear as he rose to the bait like a true victim. I was told that he was an only child who was molly-coddled by his parents, over-protected and so unable to stand up for himself. He seemed utterly pathetic. A small lunatic was taken out by the Head of Year 8 shouting, "That teacher's a knob". I wondered at this antiquated label.

I came back home feeling destroyed and incapable of doing anything save slump down in an armchair to contemplate my barrel of curses. Round the country I could see the thousands of other knowledge merchants nursing chronic psychological injuries. In shame I reach for the gaspers. Without my nicotine fix where would I be?

Fortunately I am almost teetotal so I don't grab for the bottle. A cup of tea will suffice as will the wonderful silence of my house, which has replaced the hellish classroom din. Today is best forgotten. The trouble is that tomorrow will be equally stressful.

It's music cover again going from classroom to classroom. I find myself in room 10 upstairs in the tatty turn of the century building. This room is usually occupied by a serious-looking teacher with glasses. He looks ground down by administrative burdens. At least the supply people don't have to fill in reports, mark exercise books, check off curriculum tasks, attend staff meetings, volunteer for after-school activities, take part in the Drama Department's production of Oliver etc.But you have to put up with the noise at all times. Today some forward sort of girls demanded a CD player so that they could play Eminem. "We'll do it quietly, sir, we'll work hard then." Sometimes it's like that. You can almost relax even if you have to keep a beady eye open to prevent things going outta control. You may also have to watch out for some stern management Johnny coming in unannounced as the muzak blares out. I watched some kid at the back of the room playing around with the computer chairs while others turned on computers despite being told not to.

"I couldn't care a damn," Christopher Brandon informed me as I wrote his name down on the temporary register. I could appreciate his sentiments. Then it was break time with the staff pretending they were somewhere else. Mohammed the ex-Egyptian and fellow supply teacher looked depressed. Who wouldn't be with only the odd day of paid shouting and as the summer approached you could be sure that the work would dry up completely? Mohammed wasn't a happy man nor would you be if you were well educated and over-qualified and reduced to dealing with social disintegration on a minute-by-minute basis. The lunch break was too short and there was nothing in the way of culinary delights to make the 40 minutes a pleasant interlude. Staff munched their sandwiches in the staff room; anything was better than a school dinner in the world of contracting-out. There was a lot of hot air about the need to encourage children to have a healthy diet but if you look at the stuff on sale – chips, burgers, and stodge of all kinds – it is only too obvious that school catering is price-driven with slops the order of the day. I checked my mobile to hear that there was a day of supply English the next day. This was a daily rate non-existence of formalized exploitation. The local management of schools initiative (LMS) had marginalized supplies even further by contracting out supply cover to agencies. Whereas in the past supply teachers were paid by County Hall at officially sanctioned pay rates, now you had to accept agency employment. These agency robbers were often ex-teachers who couldn't stand another minute of teaching so decided to exploit their colleagues. More often than not, agencies took almost 30% off a teacher's pay as commission. It was manifestly unfair but nothing could be done to correct the injustice, which was naturally approved by an indifferent government. Welcome to England and Wales.

(There are no supply agencies in Scotland)

After my lunch of bits of cheese and a banana there was more nonsense to endure. I was in room 2 with Year 9. The room was far too small to accommodate the class in comfort. I looked at the notice on the wall with a greeting from somebody called Mrs.Bloggs. "Have a nice day," said Mrs.Bloggs. This poster was part of English work focussing on the use of capital letters. I wasn't having anything of the sort as Callie and Gloria needed to "find their bags" which "we lost in the Drama Department". Kids wanted any excuse to get out of the classroom and who wouldn't try it on? I always did myself when I was at school. I skulk behind my Specsaver glasses and middle-aged man expression as the noise keeps going till 2.45 p.m, the goodbye time. There wasn't much to look forward to afterwards. More than likely I would have a bad night with an upset stomach, head churning after the day's self-denial and mortification. Not that it was bad always – sometimes you were pleasantly surprised such as the time I went to the Scillies for two weeks. This was a good one, flying over to St.Mary in the helicopter, staying in a bed and breakfast during the week and flying back to the mainland at the weekend. It was November so the islands were deserted and I enjoyed fine walks after school along the rugged coastline. The school was quite OK since the children there had not been polluted by the poison on the mainland. It was a throwback to an idyllic yesteryear. I could see why Harold Wilson would want to retire to such a pleasant place. But most of the time it was bad and getting worse by the hour. Even middle class places could be pretty hard going but again there were exceptions. I didn't mind St.Ives or schools in Truro and Tregony, for example, where you could put on an illustrated talk on whatever subject and not be interrupted. I thought back to the Hitler film on the Bristol Channel. Was I any better as a teacher now than back then? Were the kids any worse at that time? I think on balance things generally are worse but I'm just the same person as I was in 1976, a few years older that's all. Education is a wacky world in any case, run on a wing and a prayer, however much the politicians pretend to make it like a factory operated by robots.

You are always pathetically grateful when you have what passes for a "normal class". That means that the class do what you want them to do, behaves properly and works quietly and co-operatively. I managed this every so often. I strode into room 10 shouting out that the class had to do Act 1, Scene 3 of Macbeth when in fact they were supposed to do a quiz on "Of Mice and Men". I must have read Steinbeck more than thirty years ago so I felt like the big galoot Lennie after my faux pas. The class seemed quite understanding though, much to my appreciation. So the hormonally askew people in the classroom could be human too it appeared. On this particular day I was lucky. I had an amazingly quiet Year 11 that actually remained silent for a French test. The normal scene was people talking out of turn and asking how to answer the questions. So full marks to Year 11. After this silent miracle I continued to be amazed by a Foundation French group who were also having a test. They were quiet throughout and I was able to go over the questions at the end. Although they were not very bright they were at least amenable. Just as I was beginning to be lulled into a false sense of security I was pulled back to reality at the last lesson. This was RE, an unpopular and woolly subject – the class weren't exactly thrilled with Buddhism. Streetwise kids shouted across the room as I tried in vain to take the register. It was hopeless. A stern PE mistress was summoned to browbeat the mob. She hauled out a boy after he called her a "bum". A girl was called a prostitute by a cretinous crowd of yobs as I reflected on the Guatama's message of compassion.

Now I could escape for the weekend and reassure myself that I was a nice guy with my heart in the right place. I couldn't possibly be doing the job to get rich so why was I doing it? Did I really care? Nowadays I found it impossible to reconcile my earlier idealism over the importance of education, my own rebellious approach to school and the rowdy shambles that happened every day. There was a big difference between the totally authoritarian nature of school in 1960 and the present weak and blinkered reality of so-called progressive viewpoints. The old way may have been draconian but it worked. The new way is wishy-washy and doesn't work. I see no reason why well-intentioned people like me should be subjected to ridicule and invective without the slightest chance of redress. I'm not a champagne socialist and think that it was a serious mistake to abolish grammar schools and do away with selection. If you want to learn something you will learn much better with people of the same level of ability. Bright people get bored by the endless concentration on slow learners. Nobody learns anything in the mixed ability set-up as in any case the teacher will spend half the lesson trying to deal with mindless disruption. Nothing will work as long as policymakers deliberately ignore the true facts that schools are encouraging yob culture. Manners, basic politeness and acceptable behaviour are disappearing fast under the influence of Eastenders, Big Brother and celebrity bores. Refusing to deal effectively with off the wall behaviour as a matter of policy is both irresponsible and socially destructive. It is no use just telling teachers to chill out and listen to sermons on equality of opportunity, gender issues, racism and so on. Teachers are tired of being told what's wrong with them. It's what's wrong with the whole purpose of state education that needs a complete reappraisal. Schools just keep crime off the streets and in-house. Why add to the statistics by going public with what is really happening? All you ever hear about is the wonderful increase in A grade passes when everybody knows that the standards of general literacy have plummeted. Nobody reads books for pleasure, only for the exam. Concentration on sideshows fails to hide the collapse of social structure in the classroom. I know all about unsupportive parents, insolent children of all ages, unhelpful management, boorish busybodies from Ofsted and the assumption that it's all the teacher's fault. It isn't. You try and see how you can tolerate 6 hours of noise and confrontation every day of the week and still stand up. The mess has trickled down to junior schools as well so don't believe that your average class of 8 year olds is populated with little angels holding hands as they walk in line. More likely the teacher is dealing with a battle between whites and blacks, Asians and Arabs while proper control over events has vanished into meaningless paperwork. Don't kid yourself that it will all be alright in the end. It won't since government isn't really interested in public services under the post-Thatcherism agenda. How many ministers send their children to the lousy dustbin up the road? There is something seriously wrong and nobody is prepared to consider the solution in a class-ridden society. The holy willies in Downing Street make sure that they are just fine thank you; so don't expect any developments from the self-righteous politicians. Calculated under funding of state education sector inevitably makes the private sector feel pretty self-satisfied. Why don't we just start again, abolish the toffy-nosed establishments like Eton, Fettes College, Harrow and other bastions of privilege so that everything can be part of state education. The best of the private sector should be incorporated into a meritocratic state system with a clear division between academic and technical education. Otherwise the cause is completely lost. Language teaching has been more or less curtailed while the main emphasis in schools is on dumbing down and vacuous positive profiling. The "good morning colleagues routine " which happens every morning with the whole staff gathered for the morning briefing isn't exactly inspiring either. Tomorrow and the day after that will be exactly the same as today. I know.

My nervous breakdown was coming just that bit closer as I drove back to work feeling absolutely awful. It was musak again! Crazy boys fought each other in the middle of the classroom as they gave the finger to a teaching assistant. Order of a sort was restored but it was an uneasy truce with the headbangers. Back in the staff room the dishevelled Head of Maths muttered to a waspish-looking female colleague that all the "mentals" were timetabled for a particular lesson. I buried my face in the "Guardian" – the world was burning as usual. I flashbacked to the Year 8 Mentals. I asked one moron if I could get him a psychiatrist or else get him some medication. Unfortunately irony was lost on mentals so I was reduced to shouting insanely that "you are ridiculous". But of course it was me that was utterly absurd. Michael Mounce then felt able to throw a banana at me before leaving the classroom without permission as the cartoon teacher taught on. The Head of Musak comes in wearing her unfashionable floral trousers to get apologies from goons who have been disruptive. "Sorry, sir for wasting your time" they mumble sheepishly. "Sorry, Miss for being bad" they insincerely apologise as she tells them that they are going to lose thirty minutes off their lunch break.

The mobile rang. "Hello Paul," I said. It is Paul from the agency but the class think it is Paul the Deputy Head. I don't disillusion them but then say it was my grandfather.

"He'll be 150 next week" as I told some clowns misbehaving at the back of the class that they were "wind-up merchants". "I can always tell the wideboys after thirty years in the job " I said stupidly. They seemed to appreciate my sense of humour as I gave them a rendering of Jim Reeves country and western song, "Big John". I was a performer. Then it's Year 7 Geography with a noise level at top volume. This was impossible rubbish making me feel my age as job satisfaction crashed into the minus stakes. You start off with the best of intentions to be friendly and accommodating but in five seconds you are shouting madly to keep order. Some days every lesson is a major confrontation with trainee fascists in the making. There was a grim science lesson for example where the atmosphere was actually violent and threatening and I don't scare easily. A girl was being picked on for being different – she was "on report for poor attendance and I could see why – "fucking lezzie, dirty dyke, slut!" came the shouts from the rest of the group. I reported the incident at once and sent the poor girl off to recover as I then wrote out a report that nobody would ever read. Luckily there was a support teacher present who would validate anything I said but it wasn't pleasant to be shouted at by low life. "Fucking paedophile, you could be a perv, " shouted a boy malevolently. I have no idea how anybody should respond to such an insult save object in the strongest terms. Teachers put up with this sort of thing day after day and nobody does anything about it. You're on your own most of the time.

At the beginning of lesson 2 somebody had set off the fire alarm so the whole school trooped out to stand stupidly in the tennis courts as a roll call was taken. Back in the staff room Mohammed looked as though he was being killed slowly. He had just endured a head kicking in the Music Department and had to "face the music" next lesson. It was an uphill struggle dealing with revolting characters who had no notion of decency. You could write as many disparaging comments as you liked on impossible children but the shouts and insults would continue regardless. Outside room 35 I was delighted to hear two foul youths being humiliated by senior management after I'd thrown them out for chucking books around the classroom.

"You already have a history of violence and disruption. Teachers are not in school to put up with the disgusting behaviour of children whose parents haven't taught them to behave properly." I listened to the lecture with some satisfaction as the disruptive cretins looked suitably ashamed. They were the kind of children who told you to your face that "My mother doesn't mess about – she came into my tutor group to tell the teacher that she was a load of shit." How can anybody be expected to be polite to these sorts of people? Teachers are not a bunch of self-flagellating masochists although it may often seem that they are. You find of course that the younger teachers can be very disapproving of an oldster like me. They like to imagine that they are "close to the kids" as they affect a fashionable vocabulary – The young fanatic running the RE Department at Bodmin was a case in point. I had to cover a class for her with the subject being "God." It was a Simpsons' view of the Almighty but the class weren't very interested in burning religious questions. The Head of RE started the class off with comments of "cool", "chill" and so on. Ultimately this over-identifying strategy doesn't work at all as getting too familiar with kids can lead to a catastrophic downfall. I know this for a fact from bitter experience. It is much more effective to establish a clear distance between yourself and the kids. They prefer it that way and actually expect you to perform like a tyrant. Pally teachers don't offer any challenges to resentful kids and the Uncle Friendly approach gives out a misleading message. It's like me starting off thinking that you will be a different teacher from the ones who tormented you in the days of your youth. You intend to be an approachable teacher, putting on a laidback style and showing your students that you are really different from all the other uptight gits in the staff room. But relations with pupils in an institutional setting are very fragile and at the end of the day any teacher has little significance on their ordinary lives. Anyway everybody has to grow up eventually so why pretend to be 25 when you are over 50? Like most teachers I started off with a great sense of purpose that I could make a difference. I was still an unreconstructed rebel believing in all sincerity that I was different but I'm not. I'm just another disillusioned mug left wondering how I could have been such a naïve fool. Your charges are children and you are an adult so face up to reality and do your duty. My fantasies of making a pioneering breakthrough as an educational leading light had failed me utterly. I was looking at the stark reality of the classroom as never before. Head thundering with financial pressures I was tense as wire as endless classroom disturbances insulted my dreams, memories and reflections. The young Australian had started off with a bright and open outlook but after months of madness she was beginning to crack. She couldn't wait for the term to finish so she could get on with her travels round Europe. I sympathised with her completely as I walked into another incident. A girl was standing up screaming at another girl. "You fucking slut. You fucking slut." She then tipped over a table before storming out the classroom. I could only sigh cynically as a mere man unable and unwilling to deal with female conflicts. I felt sick to the teeth with nauseating teenagers, their hostility and precocious demeanour, their ignorance and immaturity. Perhaps at home the mad children of the classroom were pleasant teenagers but as a supply teacher I wasn't going to see much in the way of their personal charms. An apple flew past my head as I spluttered in outrage at being treated like a piece of dirt.

"What's your name, sir? Your first name, sir."

"Mr."

"Mr.?"

" Yes, mister. Mr.Dullerson."

I heard shouts offside. I looked at a paper aeroplane that had landed on my desk. "O'right sir" it said. "Ur gay".

What else could I do save inwardly retreat? It was a bright sunny morning at the sports college. I was supposed to be covering PE but there was little for me to do save sit watching the keen PGCE trainee putting a Year 7 class through its paces. They are practicing some sort of jumping technique into a sand pit. I admired the trainee's competence. He knew all the names and kept the kids on their toes. Years ago I had lost any ability to behave in such a way. Anyway I wasn't a PE type. I remembered my own negative experiences at school in the PE class. I had lost my kit forever.

Instead I was teaching a hack lesson in "life skills". Was this relevant to working life or merely an excuse for keeping the school leaving age at 16 when half the school population would have been better off getting out at 13? I had no say in the matter. I had no power to change anything. I just had to put up with another chaotic Art lesson where there was no work set, no paper or materials.

"Now class it's observation drawing. Take any object and sketch it carefully." Paper aeroplanes flew about as several nutters ran about although to be fair opposition to my artistic instructions was muted. Next a French class full of "J'ai I trouve, j'ai perdu" and other delights from the present perfect tense tested the class abilities to the limit.

After that I was called over to the Withdrawal Unit. Matthew Clark sat in an isolated booth staring at an atlas. He'd been caught smoking. . I read more dull pages from the "Guardian". The afternoon consisted of managing a class who had to watch an out of date video of "Great Expectations". Nobody was remotely interested including myself so for the sake of peace after 30 minutes somebody switched over the cricket. This seemed the best way to make life bearable although often you could get hauled up if you didn't follow the set work. If it was inappropriate and the weather was stiflingly hot I reserved the right to change the format. The thing was that you could always get caught out, quite unaware of what you had done wrong. I was wondering why the "sports college" hadn't been in touch. As usual information had to come from second-hand sources. It transpired that "there had been complaints" from a pupil as well as an adult. On further enquiry I was told that the mother of a disruptive child had complained that I had called her son "deaf". I remembered a day when an impossible boy had refused to do anything I asked. In exasperation I said "Are you deaf?" It turned out that he really was deaf but asking such a question was a perfectly legitimate way of trying to get somebody to follow instructions. How was I supposed to know the boy was hard of hearing? What annoyed me was the acceptance of unjustified allegations by school management with no attempt being made to discuss the problem with me, the teacher. As always the supply teacher was a sacrificial lamb without rights or recognition. A familiar tactic by the management was to toady to pupils and also parents. PR was much more important than admitting that there might be more than one side to a story. After any incident it was more than likely that some senior management figure would invite the culprit for a man-to-man discussion. "Let's look at this issue as mature people," he or she would say, making it apparent that what had happened in the classroom was over and done with. The hapless teacher naturally didn't have any say in the matter and as for a supply teacher forget it. Later I succeeded in getting back on the sports college supply list but only after stating my case in no uncertain terms.

Further exposure to the delights of "music" tried my patience. It was a video lesson – "Lord of the Rings". By now I'd seen the video more than ten times with different classes. Deranged children shuffled and fidgeted. A girl ran crying from the classroom after being kicked unmercifully by bullies. The misguided policy of "inclusion" meant that the most disruptive elements enjoyed free reign. The unrealistic goal of "whole class teaching" guaranteed continuing disturbance to lessons. In room 24 a crowd of kids were sitting in sullen silence. A teaching assistant was instructing the trainee criminals on how to assess a film in terms of "violence, sadness and other emotions." I switched on the Lord of the Rings for the nth time. Only one boy watched.

I was wasting my time but at least I was saving myself from penury. Classes blurred into one another. I saw myself in yet another lunatic "French" class. Sour-faced teaching assistants wanted me to clamp down on troublemakers but what sort of authority did I have? I felt that the TAs didn't like supply teachers. Maybe they thought that supplies got paid a fortune, a common misconception. I came home from the meaningless day to listen to platitudes from some government spokesperson on the radio. The implication of his remarks was that standards were markedly improving. It was just more government propaganda which I dismissed out of hand. As a matter of course nobody would listen to my opinions on the subject. Really I thought the content and standard of lessons hasn't improved at all since 1976 when the inspector called to criticize my lesson before showing the Hitler film. Britain seemed to have an unhealthy obsession with the Nazis as I was called into supervise a PGCE student taking the History lesson. On the wall were the unpleasant slogans of the Third Reich.

It seemed as though time had stood still since Mr.Plonkton had ripped into me for supposed incompetence. I rested my case as far as the curriculum was concerned. I hadn't written it and would teach anything at all as long as I got paid for doing so. But I found bigoted and parochial outlooks hard to take and there were lots of blinkered perspectives. Gone were the days when teachers keenly discussed politics with any interest. Stuck in the backwaters of petty nationalism little England was characterized by anti-Europeanism and ludicrous stereotypes of life beyond the shores of perfidious Albion. Maybe repression and Puritanism was everywhere in the world but idiocy was permanently present in the average British school. I had sunk into sink schools, crushed by a mindless routine and an absolute lack of purpose or stimulus. Most of the time the kids regarded you as a moron. A boy asked me to mark his Maths work. At the age of fourteen he couldn't work out that 7X4=28. I pointed out that his answers were wrong. "No they're not" he shouted rudely. "I'll prove it on the calculator". I was furious and asked if he thought I was indeed a moron. "Yes you're a moron" he spat at me as I told him go back to his seat and learn some manners. Later on an authority figure came to deal with the crowd of hyenas This is how you pass the time – shouting and being insulted as impending social collapse looms. You get tired of the treadmill without having a decent holiday because you can't afford one. You are stuck in an institutional land of the gloomies as your life is reduced to mere survival.

There's not much to get excited about as you keep arriving at different schools and a predictably frosty welcome. Some school secretaries can be especially off-putting.

At one place I went to the first lesson but I wasn't required. Sensibly I vanished to the staff room to read the "Independent" for a change. For lesson 2 it was a chaotic PE something or other. Dutifully en route to my fun hour I was suddenly confronted by the bisom in the office. "Mr.Dullerson," the secretary said stiffly, "I went down to E8 where you were supposed to be teaching but you weren't there." I resented being treated like a naughty boy as I retorted that I hadn't been required. "Oh I see," the bisom's face relaxed into an insincere smile. At PE all was insane with screaming kids and nothing obvious to do. As a gale blew boys hit balls round the tennis court outside as I walked about trying to look important. More yobbish kids swore and fought, oblivious to anybody or anything. At last I was able to dismiss the tennis champions and run to a ghastly French class.

"Draw the pictures of les vetements and label in French. Colour in nicely, please." I instructed as a girl grabbed my briefcase and threw it about. When I remonstrated with this monster she jeered, "What can you do about it?" Indeed what could I do save contemplate Doom. I went down into the bottomless well of the supply ocean. It was hard work losing my temper every quarter of an hour. You were often put in really silly situations and rudely treated by the person responsible for supply cover. You were just expected to accept being treated as a dogsbody. I sat in the assembly listening to some hierarchical greybeard crapping on incomprehensibly on some worthless topic. The Headmistress sat like a scowling owl watching like a hawk.

I couldn't identify with any of it apart from the weekly pittance. I was used to noise and mayhem of course but it didn't get any better. I arrived at the E5 hut for an afternoon registration. Inside E5 I saw kids covering the blackboard with insulting comments on some other unfortunate teacher. I shouted pointlessly as a grim-faced woman came in to sort the swine out. Whatever way you looked at it you were on a loser. I was walking along a corridor in some dustbin school when a girl started yelling "Homosexual, homosexual, homosexual!" I am not that way inclined myself but her insult reminded me of when I was fifteen. I'd been out with a girl called Phyllis Stewart of the same age. “You’re a poof!” she mocked after I’d failed to establish any chemistry between us. Next day at the Glasgow High School the story had got around. I was tormented unmercifully by the bullies who had probably never been near a girl. Not being gay I don’t really understand what it must feel like to be so vilified and as a non-gay I object to the unprovoked insults that are the daily lot of outcasts like myself. You become more of an outsider with the passing of the years. You might as well just be some sort of minder rather than some intellectually inclined weirdo. It was an “events day” so teachers had to take their classes out for the bicycling section. An American, sporty sort of character in a tracksuit gave kids a self-serving lecture about his successful bicycle manufacturing business. Still listening to his stuff was just that bit more bearable than enduring some dreadful Geography lessons. These required all my diminishing energy to even keep the unwilling pupils in the classroom. I was in the last stages of exhaustion. There was an urgent need to change direction and do something different. There was nothing more certain than change I assumed but nothing was ever straightforward. I knew that I was out to lunch after years of supply teaching. I had become just one more grumpy old man lost in laborious self-analysis. Teaching abroad though might prove an opportunity to rediscover my initial enthusiasm for the marginalized profession.

I asked what I was doing with my life. Did I have any plans for the future? Was there a future? Was life really better in Kuala Lumpur? Perhaps it would be better instead to stay in Edinburgh, get a steady job and settle down. Did I want to pay off my mortgage? Did I want my marriage to stay together? What did I really, really want? Was I going to retire to Spain at 50 only to get burgled a week after I’d settled into my expensive villa? Did I want to lose all the gold I’d wasted ten years earning in the Empty Quarter? I had no idea at all. I just wanted to travel, see the world, and live a little. How was I to know that I would end up in Limboland? Time flies past and unless you write that novel you’ll never do it. So I took the plunge and flew off into the sunset.

..........................................................................................

# LIBYA 1983

Back in Hawally I had nothing else to do save mull over past events. There were two more shitty weeks till Ramadan. I took myself back to Libya in 1983.

Eventually the Libyan visa came through from the London Bureau. I'd spent fruitless weeks trying to get air tickets but all to no avail. I got past the mad doorman at the Bureau in St.James Square and entered the apparently Kafkaesque world of Libyan diplomacy under siege. Paranoid Libyans sat glued to a dozen TV screens, mortally afraid of an impending attack by hostile forces. I'd first heard the word Libya mentioned at Horsmonden when it was suggested to me that I should apply to the English Department at the University of Al-Fateh in Tripoli. In September 1983 I wrote to Dr.Mohammed Ferhat asking for a job in the English Department. Soon I received a contract from somebody called Haji Ali Dhan with the good news that I had been appointed to the position of Assistant Lecturer at the grand salary of 5250 Libyan dinars, theoretically worth around $18000 at the unrealistic official rate of exchange. I was delighted, accepted immediately and looked forward to a swift departure from my old way of life. But getting there was not so easy due to the difficulties of obtaining an entry visa. A colleague told me that Libya wasn't a welcoming country but if I could tolerate the conditions then there was money at the end of it. Eventually I received a contract from Tripoli with a request for the names and passport numbers of family members and myself to be telexed. This I did at vast expense but nothing happened. I got tired of endless waiting and making fruitless phone calls to the People's Bureau. I drove up from Bristol to London to find out what was happening. Nobody had heard of my existence when I got there. I walked in to be frisked by the mad doorman who enjoyed his work with his metal detector. I was asked to sign the visitor's book then walked past the chain-smoking Libyan paranoids to be ushered into the visitor's waiting room. I filled in the visa card, which was in English and Arabic. Some shabby Tefl types looked up as I entered. I was hoping to join their crew and would get to know them well over the coming months. I explained to various Libyan officials that I wanted to obtain visas for wife, child and myself and be issued with air tickets to Tripoli. But I was told it was not possible to see the person with whom I thought I had arranged a specific appointment.

"You are Dr.Dullerson? Welcome."

"Yes I have a problem. I'm supposed to meet the Cultural Attaché at 2 p.m. but he's not here."

"Yes.Mr.Mahmoud is a very busy man."

"Well so am I."

"Can you help?"

"Of course I am very helpful."

"I'm sure you are."

"In London everybody is helpful."

"Quite so."

"There is no problem."

"But there is. I want to get to Tripoli as Al-Fateh University has offered me a post. The Cultural Attaché was going to discuss the visa and air tickets with me."

"You must see Mr.Sulliman in the Visa Section. Maybe your tickets are already waiting at Libyan Arab."

"Bukra, bukra, mush mumkin al-youhm " was the response from Mr.Sulliman (expressions well-known to Middle East travellers – tomorrow, tomorrow, not possible today) But I insisted on being seen by somebody. The mad doorman engineered a meeting with the Chairman of Garryounnis University in Benghazi who was interviewing candidates. I was shown into his office as his telephone rang. The Chairman answered a shrill female voice at the other end of the line that apologized for bothering him but there was a Mr.So and So who had to speak to the Chairman "urgently". The caller was casually informed that the matter was not "urgent" and in any case he was not available, even as he sat right in front of me. Pleasantries were exchanged before I was shown out to see another gentleman. The Libyans are a very courteous people as a rule and place a strong emphasis on formal politeness even if external form completely obscures the reality of situations. Eventually I left my passport and qualification Photostats with the Visa Section before departing. I took with me the advice of the mad doorman to come back on Saturday morning. There was much winking and nudging on his part as he told me that "these people don't like to be hurried."

After two months of useless waiting I knew what he was on about. The saga seemed endless. As an impatient Westerner I would have to learn the undoubted Arab virtues of stoicism and patience, sterling qualities with which I was not naturally endowed. One fine day in November I returned to the Bureau where I found authorized visas waiting. I was smilingly instructed to go down to Libyan Arab Airlines in Piccadilly. I parked the Ami on a single yellow line somewhere off Regent Street then walked to the office. I observed with interest the large police presence in central London due to a CND demonstration that day. At Libyan Arab I met with more frustration on being told by a charming Lebanese girl that tickets were deposited there for collection by visiting academics. It was mainly medical staff that was dealt by her office. Sometimes, the girl continued in impeccable English, tickets were sent to the Bureau for collection so her advice was to return there. I got back to the car and cursed as I saw the parking ticket on my windscreen. Back at the Bureau I went straight to the Visa Section. After much difficulty I was able to see a person of apparent influence who directed me to the Cultural Section upstairs. The whole place reminded me of scenes from Escher's paintings. I was lost in a maze. On the third floor I was told that I should pay my own fare and be reimbursed but I said that this would not be possible. I didn't want to be stuck with unchangeable Libyan dinars. I had already written to Tripoli protesting about this unreasonable request and followed this up with another expensive telex asking the university Academic Appointments staff to send me air tickets. My letter to Tripoli merely produced a telex a fortnight later telling me that I should pay my own airfare tourist class and be reimbursed. I didn't know anything about the Arab world at this time so my reaction to all this was rage and desperation. I had put a lot of effort into getting this job and the prospect of having my Third World revolutionary perspective shattered at the last moment was devastating. My paper radicalism did not take kindly to bureaucratic complications especially when I had set my sights on a personal meeting with the Colonel himself. I was a real greenhorn. I thought there was something interesting about the tarnished mystery of the Mahgreb. The shabby world of Tefling hadn't quite struck home. I was intrigued by the prospect of going to Libya in order to earn a large tax-free salary and to turn my back on the squalid supply scene. The world of "linguistics" still held a measure of intellectual fascination in the days before the MA in Linguistics became commonplace and the RSA Diploma was quite rare. I remained in a frame of serious academia that had ceased to exist around 1926 when my father had graduated from Medical School. My conditioning had made me feel that academic attainment was the only virtue in a world of vice; so it was inevitable that I would end up in the JAM. Old hippies dealt with their emotional confusion and became Third World professors.

I left the Bureau, my fantasies of meeting up with the American President of the RIF Corporation at the Kabir Hotel in Tripoli taking a fatal blow. It seemed that after all I was not going to be an important member of the expatriate community. My dog-eared copy of the Green Book seemed to be a passport to yet another cul-de-sac. The communications between Tripoli and London were extremely messy but then I was firmly stuck in my Western frame of reference. I was pretty naïve, my unschooled mind boggling at the indirectness of the Arab mentality and I became convinced that the Third Social Theory was a sort of Islamic psychosis. It hadn't occurred to me of course that under Gadaffi Libya was not especially Islamic and that an anti-colonial perspective such as his was well founded. My patronizing outlook disguised a perspective of colonial anthropology and ignorance. I didn't realize at the time how completely Western I was but experience would soon make me face up to my narrow post-hippy persona. I had not yet learned that all things are possible if Allah wills it. Eventually Allah intervened, the tickets arrived and we were bound for Tripoli courtesy of Libyan Arab Airlines, one of the worst in the world.

The plane touched down at Tripoli International Airport. The temperature in North Africa was pleasant in contrast to the big freeze in London but I was full of trepidation over my chosen course of action. The accommodation turned out to be less of a problem than I had feared. Unlike some people who ended up in a tiny room next to the lavatory in a student building, we were lucky enough to be given a large room with a balcony and bath on the sixth floor of the inappropriately named Libyan Palace Hotel. Self-catering apartments were supposed to be available at a later date but in the event these never materialized. Room 623 was to be home for the foreseeable future and what a home! Libyan soup, coca cola and greasy room service were alleviated by an abundance of oranges. People from every country in the world were packed into this downmarket flophouse, all of them on the quest for foreign currency.

"Welcome to Jamahariya, Doctor" said the Fat Man at the Palace reception desk. Welcome to the mainline saloon, I thought, along with wife and family.

"I don't like being in a Muslim country with my Jewish background" my wife said.

All the Jews had left Libya after the 1967 June war. It was through her that I managed to get to the JAM in the first place. She had even married me in order to share my venture into madness. The Palace had dirty corridors where cats wandered freely and cat shit was everywhere. But it was a meeting place for the University's avant-garde. Its tacky restaurant with trachoma-plagued waiters made an ideal setting for the bizarre conversations that were always going on.

"Awfully bright man " snarled Dr.Barry Harmer, the self-styled Professor of English at Al-Fateh University. This was his standard phrase, which assessed an acquaintance for his competence in medieval poetry. I first met him in his flat in Maida Vale when he had told me about life in the JAM. His weasel face and scornful camp style combined to produce a colourful line in invective. Men tolerated him as he was very amusing. Women hated him. He made it plain that he disliked children.

"Unspeakable Pakistanis were removed from a plane, after which the foul-smelling interior was fumigated. Gadaffi thought that as the CIA were backing Zia then all Pakis were dangerous enemies. Being Mohammedans they thought they thought they would be treated as brothers in the great Libyan Peoples Jamahariya. But that's typical of so-called Muslim brotherhood. Islam is hardly good for a dead dog, let alone the belief system of millions of deluded fools."

A Libyan opposite began to make objections. "Oh go away! " said Harmer making a fly swatting motion. Harmer was without shame. As Professor of English he had been given a tatty flat and special living allowance that barred him from making use of the Palace facilities. But the professor was mean and wily. "I've come out without cash," he would say to a new staff arrival. "Perhaps you can front me a few dinars." He never repaid any debts, as all that mattered was the holy cause of Barry Harmer. Two Irish lorry drivers arrived one day from Algeria with a load of meat and crates of whisky hidden in the carcasses. Harmer cornered them as they were sitting at breakfast so that he could bum a meal off them. As a supremely talented scrounger, he was soon yabbering away like an old friend to the shell-shocked drivers who were looking ahead to several dismal weeks kicking their heels in the Tripoli rubbish heap

"I can introduce you to Gadaffi's interpreter. He likes the booze so if you can cut me in on the deal I can set up some good business for you." Harmer said. Here he was, a man who had been enjoying free lunches for more than fifteen years. He did very little in the way of teaching and took advantage of each and every situation. Harmer recruited various desperadoes in London although I had got in by the back door. Along with Harmer I joined fat Amanda Green from London, her friend Rose from Australia, dual national Benny from Nigeria and the UK, Noel Tumilson a refugee from bankruptcy in Belfast and Harry Conlan, a slave to the British banks. There were also two Canadians, John and Deborah who had been enticed to the JAM after hearing about the revolutionary paradise. Disillusion set in almost immediately as the news got bad from the outset with the announcement that the remittance in foreign currency was to be cut from 90% to a miserable 50% (later to be revised to 60%). Harry's face crumpled with this body blow, which put his dreams of paying off his creditors seriously in jeopardy. "90% was just about acceptable, 75% barely tolerable but 50%!" he screamed. As it turned out he didn't last the course and nobody was surprised when he did a runner after the mid-term break. Noel too was upset at what he found as he had been in Libya during the golden 1970s. He was clearly shocked at the marked deterioration all round. Even the price of bootleg whisky was up to around £50 a bottle. Money was the sole topic of conversation, passing the endless hours staring out into nothingness. Many people arrived on an optimistic note such as the Indian doctor laughing about the cost of corruption in India. But Libya was not the anticipated Promised Land as most people found out after several months of the Jamahariya experience. After the show of togetherness at the beginning we all went our separate ways. The women in particular turned their backs on their downbeat male colleagues, probably as means of survival.

"Darling, my baby I come to your room," said a voice on the phone in Amanda's room. She was pestered with obscene calls till she eventually moved out of the Palace along with her haughty friend Rose. The two of them got well in with the flash Head of Security and his oily cronies and this arrangement gave them a free hand. Now there were no social meetings with the other teachers thus showing how non-existent relations were between Europeans. Noel retired to drink for the twenty-week endurance test while Benny busied himself with camp conversation at the Palace coffee bar.

At the Al-Fateh Science Department everything was in a state of disrepair, as was everything else in the country. The huge complex of tatty Italian buildings housed expensive equipment that was totally ruined. The language lab where I taught was in a sorry condition with miles of old tapes littering the dusty floors and broken windows letting in the desert winds. I found myself dealing with very large and unmotivated classes. "Now did you see Ahmed last Fall on the sidewalk of East 22nd Street" asked the out-of-date textbook. The textbook had been left behind with the departure of the Americans who had been running the show in the recent past. Since they had gone the efficient American system had been replaced by mayhem. There was no consistent decision-making process, as all power seemed to lie with popular committees. The daily administrative routine was a paper chase with authorization for the simplest request signed in triplicate. American English wasn't what I had in mind but I was learning rapidly about Tefling. There were many gaps in my knowledge and I had an unrealistic view of how things should be done. I had a grand vision but lacked the ability to focus on small details. I found that the East European teachers were much more committed to teaching English by encouraging what seemed to me to be endless and futile debates on obscure grammatical points. Clearly this was a way of making students use the language but in my stupidity I didn't appreciate this sort of thinking. I was a native speaker who didn't need a laborious analysis of grammatical structure and nuance but the students had Arabic as their first language. They had learned it by rote and clearly needed a guide to first principles. My approach lacked concentration on essential details, a misguided strategy that guaranteed trouble. This came soon enough in the form of the Libyan Co-ordinator who didn't seem to co-ordinate anything. Taher Gubia had spent years in the USA but was a dedicated anti-American. He hated the West and especially the Western academic conmen who were now earning four times his salary and being paid in dollars. His attempts at humour seemed ridiculous while I was annoyed that Taher appeared to treat me like a clerk. John and Deborah felt the same way as they popped their Valium and wore jeans although they somehow managed to avoid Taher's displeasure. This was despite their stated antipathy for Libya, Libyans and the pure bullshit of the teaching as such. John had been told to rewrite an exam since he had set the standard too high so that all the students had failed. Nobody could possible fail in the Arab world was the message. He did as he was asked but under protest. His aspirations to be a world authority on the copula and the gerund hit stony ground. He was forced to face up the dull reality of doctoring the results; just as his friend Dr.Bahati discovered that nobody was interested in his proposed talk on Blake's view of Creation. Ethnic minorities like Indian Canadians were more than likely a despised breed in Canada and even more so in the politically incorrect JAM.

Still it was nice to be addressed as "Doctor" by students and colleagues, a bit better than MA. This pleasant state of affairs wasn't to last though. It was the last day of the miserable winter semester. My three hundred students had finished their rigged mid-year examination. To me it appeared like a repeat of the supply scene but of course it wasn't. My wife and I were going to Malta that evening for a vacation. I was dreaming of Valetta as I walked into Taher's office. My carelessly marked scripts consisted of students who followed different disciplines – Medicine, Dentistry, Vetinary Science, Computer Science and so on. Taher hadn't bothered to mention to the students that they should write their names in English CAPITALS as few staff could read Arabic letters. I handed the papers over to Taher who glanced briefly at the pile of bumf then threw them on the floor. "This is useless", he yelled. "I followed your advice on the marking scheme". I answered back. "The names don't match the subjects!" he yelled. "Look, I've tried my best. Anyway I object to being spoken to as if I was a clerk. This was an unwise comment.

"Oh Christ, I've really boobed here " I thought as Taher suddenly exploded with rage.

"Don't you DARE talk to me like that " he shrieked putting on an impressive Fuhrer act. "I'm going to phone up my friends in the military police at the airport. They will stop you leaving the country, arrest you and take you to jail where you will mark the papers properly." There was a stunned silence. For the first time in my life I felt really scared. Outside the sky darkened dramatically as thunder crashed and lightning flashed. In the space of a few minutes a cloudburst flooded the sand outside the Science building. "And because of your incompetence" Taher continued " I've missed my lunch. My stomach rumbled uncomfortably. So had I. Stupidly I attempted to shake the lunatic's hand but Taher turned away petulantly. Total negativity reigned between us until Taher spoke again. "If you had been working in a British or American university you would have been immediately dismissed," he said meaninglessly. Dismissed for what I wondered – insubordination?

Was I being picked on as the infidel so as to cover up his crass inefficiency? This was quite a learning curve.

Then suddenly Noel appeared – genial, urbane, unruffled and relaxed. He winked at me in conspiratorial fashion. "He's a fucking nutter. Let's sort this one out"

Hours later things were apparently sorted out with Taher full of apologies. He drove me back to the Palace where my wife was wondering if I had been arrested. "We are brothers, friends. It is very difficult. I teach at the Soviet camp to earn enough money. I've lost half my house – requisitioned by the government without compensation. You must understand." I began to understand that I was dealing with the social problems created by the Head JAM Boy. I suppose SPLAJ wasn't any worse than dozens of other post-colonial tragedies. Certainly Libya had suffered badly under the Italians but the Gadaffi regime wasn't making much progress either. "I understand what you mean," I said as I inwardly cursed Taher. I felt pleased to be a white European and didn't feel guilty about announcing the fact that I had started out as an idealist about Africa and the Third World. I had even considered calling my son Mubarak before reconsidering and so saving my favourite person from the curse of a lifetime. The only blessings came instead from a large off shore bank account but teaching wasn't the way to a fortune. It was a permanent head kicking.

On my return from Malta more bad news was waiting. The wretched exam papers still hadn't been marked properly. " These papers must be done again, " he said grimly. Kathem Hussain from Iraq took my arm. "You MUST do as he says. I will help you." I had feelings of mild paranoia. For three days and nights Kathem abandoned his interest in Oscar Wilde and James Barrie for the unappealing task of sorting out Arabic names into some sort of comprehensible English equivalent.

"Mahmoud. Mohammed. Mabrouk. Matouk"

Lines of boring names burned holes in my brain. The worse scene of all was when Taher Gubia had to be invited round for dinner at the Palace. Taher, Kathem and I sat round the table in the dining room. I watched in amazement as Kathem cut up the self-important asshole's lamb as we three doctors discussed the dull piles of pulp fact. Taher's face was expressionless as he heard Kathem announce that Saleh Al-Majid had scored 68% in the Pharmacology section. It was clear that he should have got a higher mark in Taher's view. And so it continued. I wanted to sink into the ground. It was no wonder that I failed to learn much Arabic. However the exam situation was sorted out and later I managed to transfer to the Agriculture Department where I was given a free hand. Liberated from the spectre of Taher I could now concentrate on the intricacies of organic and inorganic nutrients. My students were keen but cowed as they were afraid of being drafted into the army to be sent to Chad. Al-Fateh was full of privileged Libyans who had avoided conscription but the threat was always present. The academic year dragged on with classes often being interrupted for political meetings.

THE PARTY ABORTS DEMOCRACY
PARTNERS NOT WAGE WORKERS
THE REPRESENTATION OF THE MASSES
POPULAR COMMITTEES EVERYWHERE.

You could see slogans from the prolific writings of the great Colonel decorating the campus. The contents of the Green Book promised a wonderful new world free of the mistakes of the capitalist past. Uncle Moammer was teacher. friend and leader of the oppressed. He was at the forefront in the fight against American imperialism. He was incarnated as the spirit of pan-Arabism as immortalized by Nasser in Egypt. The propaganda effort was supported by colourful posters preaching the Palestinian cause. Credulous foreigners made a collection of his prolific writings in every language from the shop in Jamahariya Street. But it seemed that in 1983-84 there was an atmosphere of underlying disquiet under the PR hype as Popular Committees rooted out dissent.

"I am with Barclays Bank " smiled the Manager at the National Bank. Next day a new face was at the counter as I waited in an endless queue. "Where's Mr.Abubakir?"

"Not here any more". It was common for anybody not to be there any more. In the English Department staff room Libyan colleagues kept their heads down by avoiding all contemporary issues. "In Edinburgh I drank a lot of lager." Said Dr.Assaby. I wondered if he had drunk all the whisky that Barry Harmer had sold to him. "Looking at Shakespeare in the context of modern literature we can see many allegorical similarities" droned a very depressed Dr.Masoud. Outside I could hear that a "spontaneous demonstration " was in progress "by the will of the people".

"ARABYA JAMAHARIYA. ARABYA JAMAHARIYA!" But many of the participants didn't look too enthusiastic. A distressing drama was taking place. I saw a scaffold being erected and surrounded by chanting students. I shut the window. I didn't want to watch the unfortunates being strung up by the neck. The story going round was that an example was being made of two students for producing derogatory cartoons of the Great Leader who was popularly known as Dracula. Thousands of students were forced to watch the ghastly spectacle while foreign staff were allowed to leave the campus.

"In Libya there is nothing to look forward to," confided a young man to me as I got the bus back to the hotel. Nobody was listening save me, the pseudo-professor.

At the absurd and out of touch British Embassy nobody seemed remotely aware of unfolding events. Back in the UK, all the Libyan diplomats from the Bureau had been allowed to leave after a policewoman had been shot. I had gone back briefly to London for an interview so could see it all on British TV. At Gatwick the gate for the Libyan British Caledonian flight had a massive security presence. I was advised not to return to Libya because of the dangers of civil unrest. I didn't think twice about what I was doing as I needed to get paid and anyway my wife and son were still in Tripoli. On board the plane there were about five or six passengers surrounded by armed Special Branch characters with heavy guns. On the tarmac a tank held the plane in its sights before take off. On arrival at Tripoli all was perfectly normal as I stepped out into the warm sunshine. There were no security men, no tanks and no guns, just the usual Libyan shambles. But after the expulsions from the Bureau, diplomatic relations between Libya and the UK had been curtailed. I got into the Palace to watch the events on Libyan TV. Pictures showing the departure of the diplomats were interspersed with footage of brutal British police smashing into striking miners. So it was quite a surprise for Her Majesty's finest when the Embassy party to celebrate the Queen's Birthday didn't happen. I still have my invitation card. The useless British were kicked out beforehand.

There was a knock on Room 620 at the Palace. "It's the BBC correspondent from Algiers," said a voice. "Maybe you could give me a story about what's going on here."

"I couldn't. I am in a public position here." I replied testily.

But others could and jabbered freely to Kate Adie and the like in the coffee shop at the Kabir . Some vanished. Other hostages were taken. Michael Burdiner disappeared one night returning from the laundry. The story was that his students had picked him up since they suspected that he was a spy. This was absurd since he was harmless, spending his spare time at the French Cultural Institute. He wasn't a spy. He'd just been jamming for ten years too many. Along with several other British he faced a long incarceration in a room with a diet of tea and cheese sandwiches. It would take visits and representations from Terry Waite and Labour MP Ron Brown to secure their eventual release a year or two later.

"Are we all going to be arrested?" asked the native English speakers. The Chairman of the English Department, wondering why he had left Colorado, didn't think so.

"Just routine enquiries" Dr.Mohammed Ferhat assured the Tefling mugs as he reminisced on the fine years in Denver. Ferhat wasn't really interested in anything save getting the expatriates to do his work for him so that he could spend as much time as possible in his hometown of Al-Homs up the coast. My relations with him were awkward and stilted since my level of interest in the hierarchy didn't go beyond the polite and distant aspect.

"Takes no part in staff room activities, refuses advice from more experienced colleagues and although highly capable of discussion on a wide variety of subjects maintains a polite but distant attitude to other members of staff. More likely to be suited to youth work or else in the higher educational sphere…."

It was all repeats as I remembered the blabbering probation report of yore. Lacking the required spark of enthusiasm for any group situation it was hardly a surprise that once again I was experiencing the outsider scene. I wanted my cash for the minimum of effort, hardly an acceptable stance as I endured months of crushing boredom.

I caught up with Eric Butusill from the Maltese Embassy. Eric was the First Economic Secretary with political views firmly opposed to the commie crap of Dom Mintoff. He was extremely fat, smoked a pipe during Ramadan and was interested in obtaining low-level information from the East Europeans. There were a lot of Poles, Hungarians, Czechs, Bulgarians etc working in Tripoli but I knew that Andrej Kieres, a mathematics lecturer from Lublin didn't like Eric. So he wouldn't be accompanying me round to watch "Death of a Princess" and drink the Embassy brandy. Andrej like most Poles had a magnificent gallows sense of humour. He enjoyed driving as recklessly as the Libyans as it was a refreshing experience to be away from Soviet-style rules and regulations. Even if Libya was an African version of East Germany Andrej was determined to have a laugh. The phone went in his room. It was the Fat Man at reception. Andrej felt paranoid, sure that he was going to be chucked out of the hotel but he slammed down the blower with a shrieking shout of "Shukran!"It was all Shukran but even if he disliked Eric an evening at the Embassy was an opportunity to discuss money. There were a lot of worthless dinars floating about after the hard currency remittance had been cut. The official exchange rate was ludicrous so the best avenue was to go to Air Malta. They were in the business of getting rid of unwanted dinars. On Eric's advice I met an obliging Maltese in a back office who gave me a good deal. Even so Eric was a much better bet in his official capacity. He agreed to change 1000 dinars at the official rate through an Embassy account in Germany. Months later I got what was due.

As soon as Harmer was introduced to Eric he got on to the only subject.

"Do you change money?"

A sensible question of course. Time crawled past till at long last I was able to escape from SPLAJ with my stash. Getting out was a complicated business. At the university alone I had to obtain twenty-two stamps. I had to prove that I did not have any books from the nuclear engineering library, did not owe the student canteen any money or had rent to pay on campus accommodation despite having no connection with these places. It was a lesson in Arab bureaucratic style with men lying back on desks with a queue in front waiting for his authoritative flourish. I went to an office in Omar Mukhtar Street where a faceless official carefully and self-importantly opened his desk drawer. He took out a gold pen and a rubber stamp. He was obviously enjoying giving the silly kawaja the run-around as he asked me if I had settled my higher rate tax bill. "That's all been taken care of, " I spluttered. Somehow the official relented and signed yet another document to take me that bit closer to securing an Exit Visa.

It was a long race taking in the Tax Office, the Water Department, the Central Bank, the Jamahariya Bank and innumerable other destinations. The rules and regulations changed almost daily it seemed, so it was a constant effort to keep up with official whims. Libya wasn't a place where you could grease palms to speed things up so I just had to grin and bear it. The hardest thing was the money as getting paid was an extremely complicated business. Usually this involved visits over several days to different offices carrying a sheaf of papers. As I was leaving on a FINAL EXIT VISA an amazing number of documents had to be produced, in quadruplicate at a minimum. It was only the Central Bank, which had the authority to issue foreign currency, in the form of American Express travellers' cheques or a bank draft. Securing this authority was awesome in its convoluted twists and turns. There were hours of waiting with piles of incomprehensible papers in one's hand while I hoped that the bored official behind a glass screen might notice your presence. I could only curse when nothing happened and the official closed the screen, muttering "bukra" as he turned away from the desperate customers. I knew that the same thing would happen the next day and the day after that. I had to get down to the Central Bank when it opened at 7 a.m. There was always a large crowd already waiting. Eventually the pile of papers had dwindled to one and when the prized authority was finally obtained it was an anti-climax. This last remaining paper had to be presented for stamping at the Jamahariya Bank at the university. This was it I thought. However, after going all the way up to this bank I couldn't be paid there – instead I should return to the Central Bank in the morning. It was all completely mad but in due course I was given a pile of dollar travellers cheques along with a pile of worthless dinars. Now all I had to do was endure a whole month alone doing nothing during an interminable Ramadan.

Wife and child had departed for home at the end of May so I had Room 620 all to myself while ensuring that the Fat Man didn't know that Madam had gone for good.

I didn't want to be allocated to a tiny single room without air-conditioning.

It was the last days of SPLAJ. I hadn't done particularly well but on balance it had been an interesting year. Eric sent round the Maltese Embassy car with a Philippino driver to the Palace. I wanted to avoid the Fat Man, as I hadn't paid an exorbitant $100 hire for a tiny fridge in my room. I didn't want any last minute hitches. I made out that I was going off to work as usual and pretended that the suitcases I'd put down weren't mine. The driver picked them up as I walked casually through the lobby to the car. The car drove out to the chaotic Tripoli International Airport through the VIP section. A soldier saluted. Then I was on a plane bound for Malta.

Other soldiers with machine guns walked down the aisle staring hard at all the passengers. Apparently I wasn't wanted. The plane took off and I felt free, expecting never to return.

..............................................................................

# LIFE IS FULL OF REPEATS

The Tefling business has developed over the years from semi-legitimacy to tenuous respectability. If you have any interest in superficial appearances and the art of impression management, then TEFL is just up your street. Don't think you are going to get rich working for some Middle East outfit. The golden days are over but there's still a reasonable living available if you work at it. You may have to learn the hard way of course, as Tefling isn't an easy passage to the good life. Teflers are an odd bunch, exceptions to rules and are often unconventional since they are incapable of living a normal life. Tefling is filled with people you thought only existed in your imagination, cowboys the lot of them but a bit more interesting than your average commuter. In the past teaching English as a foreign language was a gentleman's pursuit, a job often done in the course of diplomatic duties or government business abroad. Now it's all professionalized along with everything else. The fixation on "professionalism" and "quality management" has taken a lot of the spontaneity out of Tefling and the market is saturated with qualified teachers. Many teachers are well-meaning types who believe that in some way they are able to negotiate their conditions of employment. Unfortunately the reverse is true since self-delusion is the source of a general inability to control the vagaries of the market. If you're not careful, then you can get exploited and line the pockets of entirely unscrupulous operators. Language schools for instance tend to pay peanuts, as salary structures are entirely unregulated. In Britain and all over Europe Teflers are paid a pittance for highly skilled and demanding work. How about working in Stuttgart at 12 Euros an hour doing 1-1 business clients. At that rate you'd have to teach 40 hours a week just to have barely enough to live on. Or perhaps you'd like to work for nothing at all at any number of summer schools all for the thrill? Teachers in this line of work tend either to be too nice, too conformist, and lazy or have failed to adjust to the reality of the modern workplace. The world doesn't owe you a living though .I realized that a while ago but didn't get round to Tefling till after a long spell in state education. I should have got into the game in the 70s when salaries in such places as Iran were astronomical. Anyway I had fantasies of being on a government mission or embarking on an anthropological expedition to a fascinating alien culture. This is what Tefling would do for me – give me a break from the mind-deadening routine of the daily bash. Like most people I had already earned the money in my head before I'd signed the contract and got on the plane. You don't consider what's involved in giving up your life to vanish to some dustbowl in the sun. You go to the Middle East to find wrecked lives – alcoholics who want to dry out but find themselves on a bootleg bender, solid citizens who spend five years earning vast sums only to find that back in Walsall the faithful woman has run off with the milkman and cleaned out the joint account. Or how about putting yourself in the place of committed expatriates who find themselves a young Thai, a woman from the Philippines or perhaps an African lady? They boast that what is necessary for a man is a young woman only to find that the love of their lives has blocked a residence visa application, taken over ownership of the property in Phuket or else gone back to work as a bar girl in the very bar where they met in the first place. Hardly a recipe for paradise.

I was still in the early stages of my self-abasement .I still thought that I could land a good job and earn piles of bread without too much commitment or effort. Getting the interviews was always easy, particularly when you were under forty years of age. Later, not so easy so you had to embellish your CV to look at all convincing in a world prejudiced against anybody over 45. But I was still employable at 35 as I listened to the great promises being made at the Allied Medical offices in London.

"It's a great job in Khamis Mushayt, Saudi Arabia. You'll be teaching Saudi soldiers in the school at King Fahd Military Hospital. The Asir region is very beautiful, up on a plateau so the climate's healthy. There's plenty to do and see and there's a really friendly atmosphere out there. Paid leave for a month every six months."

I arrived at Jeddah with a sinking heart. Crowds of robed pilgrims on the way to Mecca were everywhere. I felt as though I was on another planet. I was. It was 1984.

The first problem was the accommodation that I was expected to share. From comfortably married man status to enforced bachelor solitude wasn't fun but sharing with people I didn't know was appalling. I moved into a tacky bungalow on the hospital compound. Assuming everything was organized on a first come, first served basis, I grabbed the master en-suite bedroom. I lived untroubled for ten days till one night I was woken up by shouting.

"Fucking pisshead"

"Smashed as fuck"

I opened my bedroom door to be greeted by the sight of two hard-boiled types. Dave Tandell was Chief lab technician as he grandly announced in grating Cockney tones. Fellow teacher Roy Batty was equally vile. Then Tandell demanded the master bedroom.

"That's mine," he demanded.

"But I was here first"

"Look I've got friends in the management so OUT!"

Then I was fairly new to the game so I was intimidated. I moved my things to a much smaller room. This was a bad start to a very bad time. At the awful Training Center Batty fell out with his colleagues. "I hate teachers, fucking wallies, " he said aggressively. From the first day he stopped speaking to the wallies as he came out of his classes to sit in a corner with his back to the miserable chalkies carrying out their prison sentence. He puffed on his pipe boiling in a psychotic internal rage. I could see that Batty had severe problems connected to alcoholic withdrawal. I had to live with this madman. Quickly relations in the compound household deteriorated. Dave dominated the lounge with his crappy music with a couldn't care less attitude to his housemates. "Look this is my home. I'll do what I like" was his response to any objections to late night disturbances and a stream of visitors. By now Batty wasn't speaking to Dave either so I found myself in the position of go-between. Added pressure came once it became obvious that Dave was stealing large amounts of alcohol from the lab for brewing flash or cid, as it was known. Other chemicals were also disappearing from the lab thus putting us all at risk of arrest. Bottles of poisonous grog were stored in the fridge before being sold on to thirsty expats. If the police had raided the house everybody would have been in trouble but Batty or Dave didn't care and I was powerless. Matters came to a head.

"You're leaving" Dave said abruptly one evening.

"Leaving?"

"Yeh. I'm moving my mates in here and you're moving out. Sorry"

"But.."

"Forget it. My friends in Allied Medical have got clout."

With Batty I visited the Management Office to register our protest. A hard-faced lout in a shiny suit shrugged indifferently. A Thatcher boy with a coconut haircut.

"Don't worry boys, you'll be properly housed elsewhere

A furious correspondence followed but to no avail. A Western-hating Lebanese Housing Manager appeared to evict us. Later on I was pleased to hear that the Allied Medical CEO had been sacked for improper behaviour at party.

"You must leave," said the Lebanese.

"To go where?"

"To the Jordanian camp."

The Jordanian camp was miles away near the airport at Abha. A few miserable portakabins stood in the sand beside the main highway, which roared with traffic. A chain-smoking Jordanian greeted us.

"Willcome to the Jordanian camp."

"Uh huh."

Batty took one room. I took the other. The two of us began a life of mutual hostility and emptiness that lasted for at least four months. Silence dominated the interior of the squalid accommodation.

"Good evening Roy," I attempted to communicate.

Batty said nothing as he walked to the bedroom and slammed it in my face. When Batty was sober he was catatonic so in the absence of even a bare acknowledgement I retreated into passing endless hours watching boring Saudi TV. These were hard times. Occasionally Batty came out his shell after he'd gargled a few stiff ones. His conversation was egotistical and ridiculous. He proceeded to lecture me on my personal inadequacy.

"You're emotionally immature. I know your sensitivities but I know what I'm doing. Don't think that I don't." He bellowed out his projections at top volume.

Teachers are universally hated since the common misconception is that they don't do any work. Contrary to popular opinion teachers in the Middle East and elsewhere have the most contact with the natives. Thus they learn much more about the people and the country, unlike other expatriates like doctors and technical experts who have the good fortune to run their own show without being answerable to anybody.

A normal conversation with a roughie toughie could go something like this.

"O'right mate,Wotchyadoin here then, mate?"

"Oh I'm a teacher."

"A teacher. A fucking teacher. It's a fucking teacher."

End of conversation. The sort of kids I had endured as a supply teacher were now earning more money than me as mechanics, electricians, bricklayers and plumbers. Their attitude towards teachers was still stuck in the way they had behaved in the classroom. I hated them. No doubt the feeling was mutual.

Nobody invited teachers to the many parties that were organized by the hospital staff. Nurses need the heavy wallets of fat cat doctors out on a six-week locum for £10000 a month. Stupidly the bunch of balding chalkies stared into nothingness on £1000 a month. They worked hard for their money, smashing in their intelligence, trying to get thick, unmotivated students to string a sentence together. As soldiers in the Saudi army it didn't matter how many times they repeated the English language course. They had a good salary and a comfortable life. The English class was just something to do to pass the time. But it was fine for Al Gabrielli with his worthless degree in the Chiropractor field from the University of Denver. The Italian from Pittsburgh was on the large American salary he had managed to retain from the Whittaker Hospital Corporation of America's contract with the Saudis. Allied Medical had stepped in at the end of Whittaker's contract with a tender at half the price but Al had made sure that he stayed on at his old rate of pay. He wouldn't dream of working at the dismal British wages. He wasn't British.

"Hollywood's run by Jews" he said. This was always a good line anywhere in the Middle East where expatriates displayed their pro-Arab principles as matter of expediency. "You know, guys," he would say to his expectant classes, "I didn't think it was important that Mohammed failed to attend Sunday Schools. I don't care a shit if it's goddam Allah, Jesus or Buddha that you worship. You might as learn to say fuck the Pope. Anyway today it's simple Math and even prophets had to count their blessings. In my home town we gotta mosque, a Buddhist temple so what the hell, I'm a Catholic myself." He deliberately failed to mention the synagogue or the bar mitzvahs he had been to when he was back home on leave.

Students loved him, maybe because of his outrageous delivery. They thought he was a real live Doctor of Medicine. That's what it said on the door of his office – AL GABRIELLI, M.D. Only at King Fahd Hospital could this happen. Only Dr.Kildare and Dr.Gillespie were missing in the Saudi version of Blair Hospital. Al was never stuck for lines. "Y' know, you folks in England ain't developed like we have in the States. In America if you want to be the President of the Company you can be just that. If you want to go far try for a job with ARAMCO," he advised me. I wasn't going to go very far though with the Trainex learning program. On Al's large salary he could afford to be optimistic but at the Brit rate there was little mileage in burning ambition. Al sensibly conserved his energy by sleeping in his office, which also served as a video store. A notice hung on the door.

IN CONFERENCE DO NOT DISTURB

I looked thought the office window to see the phoney Dottore Gabrielli sprawled on his desk sound asleep. I went in. "Oh I was just looking for that video on order for ya.

Then I felt faint. Mustavbin that shish kebab at dinner. Yeah, it's in Arabic and English. If the guys don't understand the English then switch over to the Arabic. Take it easy, man."

At the end of the day there was a treat in store for the Training Center. Al was doing Bedouin dancing with his soldier students. I wondered how he could be one of the boys as I'd decided against team playing twenty years back. Little surprise that promotion was never to come my way. Eventually the miseries of the Ministry of Defence contract came to an end. It had been a rotten experience with an ulcerated duodenal ulcer making daily existence an unmitigated torture. It was only on the day prior to my departure from KSA that my condition had been correctly diagnosed. The redneck Canadian doctor, a true company man, had been incompetent as he handed out Librium, Valium, Librax and other useless palliatives just to keep an apparent malingerer out of his misery. As the plane took off from Jeddah I vowed never to return to the dreadful kingdom. There really had been nothing wrong with the students but I found that enduring the deadly dullness and loneliness of the draconian society made everything more or less impossible. Still, once out of the country and Saudi airspace I soon forgot the torture and there was a large cheque to compensate. Back in supposed civilization it only took half an hour to get back to normal, whatever that might mean.

.........................................................................................

# MORE KINGDOM OF SAUD

An invitation came to get on a place to take up a position at the Al-Jhahra Ethylene Plant somewhere near Jubail and Dhahran. This turned out to be the usual lousy contract, the standard bit of toilet paper that wasn't worth sixpence. The operators lining their pockets this time were Specialist Language Services who had a set-up in York, England. In the tacky SLS offices dowdy wage slaves worked all hours for a pittance, churning out photocopies for hack lessons. It had been SLS who had the temerity to charge huge sums to a Kuwaiti for one-to-one teaching before presenting him with a worthless certificate saying, " He has passed the course." As always I needed money but was filled with trepidation about working for old speed freaks from some unknown polytechnic. SLS did not have a good reputation among Teflers but as always I had no choice.

The east side of Saudi Arabia looked like a moon landscape filled with oil terminals, work camps, supermarkets and the usual quantity of sand in abundance. I arrived with ten other chalkies, some younger, some older but all desperate to escape from the nightmare of the UK. At the beginning of July 1986 Dhahran was hot, humid and oppressive. I looked round my new prison cell in a vast compound adjacent to yet another super-highway. The Arabian version of Butlins' holiday camps wasn't inviting. Students were living with the teachers and this lack of privacy was an added burden. I shared a corridor with my jolly colleagues who like me were experiencing in full measure a depressing solidarity of suffering under the hard hand of a bum rap. The salary of £1000 per month was totally inadequate with no allowance having been made by the vile SLS for local expenditure. Tiring of the endless diet of mutton and mush the teachers requested alternative accommodation. Home changed to another equally grotesque living environment consisting of lines of portakabins as far as the eye could see. A mosque dominated the entrance to this males only slave camp.

"Willcome to Al-Jhahra Ethylene Production Company" wheezed Mr.Shamrani, the greasy Saudi manager. "I am Director of Training and I hope you will be happy here," he continued insincerely. Clearly Uncle Shamrani was intending to work the wretched SLS mugs into the ground, taking the usual Middle East approach that quantity was infinitely superior to quality. Doubtless he envisaged eight one-hour classes per teacher per day, day after endless day. Peter French, an old Saudi hand had anticipated the possibility of exploitation so as Supervisor took upon himself the responsibility for computer operations. "Ahlan wahsahlan, kif halek, elhamdilalah, inta kuwais, Allah Akhbar " he waffled in style.

Mr.Shamrani beamed. "Well here we have an ultra-modern operation with a computer control room that directs the cracking process." There were blank looks all round. There wasn't one Chemistry "A" level among the SLS clowns. It seemed as if Al-Jahrah had assumed that all the teachers were highly qualified industrial chemists who had come to impart their specialized knowledge to bright young Saudis keen to progress in management. He must have had voluntary service overseas in mind at the money we were being paid. I should have gone back to Glasgow High School to ask M'Grunt for a reference on my debatable prowess in Chemistry. I watched Mr.Shamrani's features cloud over.

"You'll be working with my assistant, Mr.Mansour Al-Jazir who is responsible for the daily running of company affairs. "Willcome guys" said Mr.Al-Jazir in a convincing Chicago accent, "I'm from Algeria but working here in Saudi Arabia after studying at the Harvard Business School" He grinned an ambitious grin showing a set of perfect white teeth. "We have all the usual technological aids which you would expect to be a part of an advanced training department in a progressive company. There's film equipment, which will be useful in role-playing sessions, a state-of-the art language lab and of course the computer room. I presume you are all familiar with Windows?"

Oily Al-Jazir spat out the meaningless jargon in staccato tones. As I reflected on my latest journey into madness, I wondered what the fuckers expected. Language labs were useless for learning any language as nobody wanted to sit in an isolated booth mouthing grammatical drills into a microphone. Role-playing too was a cultural minefield in the Arab world as students normally expected the teacher to do everything. Further, coming from a teaching universe of plasticine, banda machines and chalk and talk I wasn't greatly enamoured by technology - I knew nothing at all about computers in 1986. Didn't these people realize that SLS has just cobbled together a few names, bought some plane tickets and done their sums? £1000 a month would only produce a bunch of amateurs. What a joke working for this lunatic company that basically just produced non-biodegradable plastic bags to pollute an already polluted world. I knew that these Third World technocrats really believed in the futuristic dream that was already morally bankrupt in 1930. I thought of a booming wartime America belching smoke in a 1941 newsreel. I knew that it was against my principles to have anything to do with the oil company nightmare but I was broke and my principles didn't come up with cash.

"Thanks for filling us in, gentlemen" Peter moved his ample frame in the direction of the Director and his assistants. Then the teaching began which was the usual load of nonsense. Badly educated and poorly motivated mummy's darlings shouted and pouted, dying to go to a disco in Brighton rather than take seriously the idealistic aspirations of the Al-Jhahra training program. They didn't seem very religious. But there was no end to the PR.

"This is our newest Progress Report Format, Mr.Shamrani". It was the weekly staff meeting where Peter confounded the Saudis with computer science. "Here on the chart is the average tonal performance per student per hour over a period of a week. You can see from the figures that all students are showing a consistent increase in ability with the sophisticated behavioural observation techniques we are employing. At present we are at maximum operating capacity in terms of vocabulary input per student as the present timetable is stretched to the limit. This is why any extra time should be allocated to homework." Peter turned out the whoppers superbly, protecting his poor teachers from the managerial manipulations of Mr.Shamrani. Here we were working our guts out for a pittance so why should we do any more than the bare minimum?

John Quinn though wasn't so smart. His pathetic, eager-to-please personality couldn't refuse any request, however unreasonable. He was scared of authority so he agreed to give Mr.Shamrani private English lessons in the evening. To do this he had to drive 60 miles south and back again with the vague promise of treble pay. Of course he didn't receive anything like this for his sterling efforts but he did enjoy the dubious privilege of currying favour with the boss. Here was a typically subservient teacher.

Rory started off with a fanatical interest in Islam and the Middle East in particular.

He behaved as if he was at a Methodist bible class. "Why do you believe in Allah?" he asked his class of clods. This was a dumb thing to ask in Saudi Arabia where it was wise to steer clear of religion, politics or women.

"Allah is our God. You should be Muslim, teacher."

"Yes, I'm very interested in religious discussions."

" Why you ask questions. You spy?"

Outside the ridiculous training department with its unused film equipment, irrelevant language lab and confusing computer room teachers discussed the empty content of the lessons. What were "Windows?" I remembered Ned Ludd and the machine- breakers of old.

"Is there any water in the jug?"

"Yes there is. No, there isn't."

"Did John meet Mary yesterday?"

"Yes he did. No, he didn't."

"Is Mr.Wilson a transvestite?"

"Yes she is. No he isn't"

"Have you seen Midnight Express?"

"Yes I have. No, I haven't."

Etc, etc.

Rory was deeply involved in his ecumenical discussions with the leading company fundamentalists. In the reserved smoking area he rolled a cigarette.

"You smoke Dagga, teacher?" leered Mohammed.

"No, I'm actually smoking a roll-up."

"Roll-up. Dagga. Drugs. Haram" Mohammed was a skilled wind-up merchant.

Rory turned pale with fear. From then on he shut himself in his portakabin, scared shitless (as well he might!) of being arrested for smoking dope. Every morning thereafter he emerged trembling with fright for work, did what was required but only communicating with his unprofessional colleagues in writing since he thought the rooms were bugged. Eventually the erstwhile Islamic student left never to return to the Middle East, his dreams of spiritual rebirth shattered beyond repair. In York he returned to his student musings and the comfort of a good toke on Saturday nights. And good luck to him too. Meanwhile the silly scene stumbled on.

"Here is the computer room. This is the main control centre for the entire plant." Young arrogant Saudis spoke in superior tones. It didn't seem to matter that they were sorely lacking in the necessary understanding of the cracking process. All the teachers had been obliged to listen to an incomprehensible lecture by the American industrial chemist on Ch1 this and Ch3 that. And we understood English at least. Still, for the Saudis, none of this mattered as they were already guaranteed a managerial sinecure for drinking coffee behind oak-panelled desks that held up a barrage of ivory telephones.

"YEAH ROGER. CONTROL TO CRACKING.ALL SYSTEMS GO" drawled a smarmy guy with dark shades and a flash uniform hiding an expensive pair of trousers.

It was all a farce. The biggest farce came when the pay cheques arrived. Instead of a tax-free salary, I had been taxed at British rates of tax with an emergency coding while National Insurance had also been deducted. My £1000 had been cut to nothing.

"What's this?" I spluttered incredulously. "I've just got £610 left after a full month's work in this asylum." Younger teachers looked up tight-lipped at this outburst. If you were 23 then this was BIG MONEY. Who cared about oldsters' financial problems? Shut yer mouth, oldster. I said my piece anyway wondering how I had got myself into this mess.

"Have a good weekend, guys," the laconic voice of the unpleasant Departmental Secretary echoed down the corridors. The professors fell out for the awful weekend carrying their plastic bags that were close to melting in the 45C heat. Did the secretary think we were still back in Wisconsin? Two days of pure nothingness were ahead. – a visit to the supermarket, then to the only public beach for a swim or else a walk through the rubbish of downtown Dhahran. With Terence Coysh I decided to check out the Weightlifting Center. We stayed for five minutes. Inside smiling Arab musclemen preened themselves before full-length mirrors. The two filthy infidels saw supreme vanity in action as one beaming Saudi admired his profile, another flexed his jaw muscles. Dead hours followed sitting in the asbestos surroundings of Portakabin City with the constant whirr of the air-conditioning. Terence Coysh assumed an important air as we sat about one evening.

"It's DR.COYSH!" he announced grandly. In the office the telephone call had emptied the room. It was his girlfriend. The Doctor was deeply involved in a heartrending affair, a standard Middle East phenomenon I knew all too well from bitter experience. Relationships fell apart due to absence, as hearts grew less fond by the hour. The doctor's frustration erupted.

"Don't you EVER speak to me like that again!" he roared at timid John Quinn who had merely asked him about the subject matter of his "doctorate". According to Terence Coysh it transpired that he had been an opera singer in Italy but had lost his voice. He was Dottore di Musica apparently. I would meet the Dottore elsewhere in the continuing Middle East saga.

After the absurdity of my pay cheque, I lost all motivation and made my excuses to leave on compassionate grounds. I had heard that my father in Scotland had been taken seriously ill. As the plane touched down at Glasgow I vowed to never again return to the region. Again I failed to keep my promise.

........................................................................................

# YET MORE OF THE SAME

An interview came up with ARA International in Guildford. I wasn't taken by the ex-forces outlook of this outfit whose director Ken Adams liked meeting candidates for interview in the offices of the Institute of Directors in Pall Mall. I just wasn't keen on more of the same.

"Do you want the job?" asked the brassy woman from ARA.

"No, I don't."

"Well, we're offering you a contract."

"Well, I'm not sure"

"It's yours."

She didn't want to lose her commission. And I didn't want to lose my expenses. Only too frequently it was "only successful candidates" that got expenses.

As nothing else had come up I reluctantly accepted but dreaded the idea of going back to Saudi Arabia AGAIN! . This time I was in Jeddah working at the ghastly Training Center of the Royal Saudi Airforce. Ostensibly I was employed by Lockheed but in reality I was at the beck and call of the inflexible Saudis. Aaaaaiiiieeee!! Lockheed compound was a large jail an hour's bus ride from the unappealing city of Jeddah. Some expats loved the place but its superficial air of modernity didn't convince me. There were hotels, skyscrapers flashing neon but behind the advertisement imagery it was the same old story – a boring pit like any other metropolis in the region. The accommodation consisted of the usual purpose-built bungalows. I had to share one with Happy Harry from Middlesborough and a depressed Archie from Grangemouth.

"I don't see why people talk against the company " breezed Harry in his bluff northern tones. "It's a good job." Harry was the photocopier maintenance man getting rich quick on an enormous salary of £800 a month. Obviously it was better than unemployment back home.

Archie drank in the seedy Lockheed bar every night. I hated the little England mentality, which demanded a Bull & Feathers pub to make people feel at home. The Lockheed place was a sordid venue packed with hard cases wearing gold medallions. I went there once or twice but gave up as I heartily disliked the British expat scene and didn't enjoy the fake bonhomie of the boozer. The training center too was a nightmare. Everything was navy blue including the walls, carpets, doors and RSAF uniforms. The course content consisted of the well known American Defense Language Institute course; a brain-damaging exercise in rote-learning.

"Is Bill from Cincinnati?"

"Yeah he is."

"Is Mirabelle from San Diego? "

"No she's from San Francisco."

Sullen Saudi Air Force personnel went through the motions but most of the older men had long ago reached a language ceiling so couldn't learn any more. The main idea was to pass a monthly test which nobody failed – a multiple choice answer scheme –

(a),(b),(c),(d),(e) Cheating was the norm and was expected. The naïve American attempted to conduct a proper examination. Generals, colonels, majors and other top brass talked constantly.

"1 (a), 2 (c), 3 (e), 4 (b), 5 (a), 6 (c) 7(d).."

"Gentlemen, please this is an examination," He was ignored. Sam wished he was back in Oregon with the Bagwan as anywhere must be better than here, although there were weirdoes who liked the lifestyle. Sam found the strain of it all too much to handle. He imagined that toxic fumes were pouring into his classroom when nobody else could smell a thing. Eventually he did a runner back to the Rajneesh Commune in Poona. Who could blame him I thought as I looked at the huge RSAF complex out of the window. Real people were involved in the C-130 program. Aircraft construction made sense – teaching Ahmed Bilko and Sultan Doberman didn't. I didn't enjoy the Lockheed punishment detail – working for one-dimensional American rednecks wasn't fun. All there was on the agenda were useless reflections on the situation as the long days dragged past. Weekends were especially empty, eating greasy hamburgers in the miserable "American restaurant" as I watched America's hometowners Square Dance and talk about their large salaries.

Jim McFetrich didn't fit in either. A wee man appeared. He looked straight out of "Oor Wullie" or the "Broons", classic Scottish comic cartoon characters. Jim had spent twenty years in Germany as an instructor in the Army Education Corps. Personal reasons brought about his resignation so he'd come to the Kingdom to earn what he imagined would be easy money. From the first day life for the wee man was hell. Culture shock afflicted his every waking moment.

"Right men!" he squeaked in a high-pitched Glaswegian accent. "ATTENTION!"

Matouk el-Mahdi and his crony Jaber looked pityingly at the Celtic madman. His earnest expression produced no end of merriment for the lazy men of the RSAF.

"You have problem, teacher," jeered Matouk who towered over the refugee from the British Forces Network Overseas.

"I'm going to report you to your Commanding Officer for insubordination, Matouk" spluttered McFetrich.

"Oh him? Mahmoud is a toilet boy from village. Nobody listens to him, teacher."

Matouk and company dissolved into helpless laughter as the man from Gorbals stamped his feet in impotent rage. "I'm going to resign!" he shouted. So every day for three months McFetrich resigned but his plea for early release was ignored by the management. Night after night he came to see me. I felt sorry for Jim in his state of nervous collapse. His wife had left him; his two adopted children had stolen his car and walked off with the proceeds. His girlfriend wanted to break off the relationship because she didn't want children and he did. He was on the phone every night so hardly made any money. He chain-smoked and looked about sixty-five although he couldn't have been more than forty. Poor Jim, a nice guy. It wasn't his fault that he couldn't adjust to the Saudi bullshit. I couldn't either even if I went through the appropriate motions.

One day Prince Sultan came to visit.

"ATTENTION!" I commanded absurdly. I was a true bammy Scot as along with my class of soldiers I stood ramrod straight. A mean-looking character with a goatee beard glanced indifferently into the classroom. No doubt the smarmy Saudi Gazette would report the non-event in detail next day. I could just imagine the treacly editorial.

"His Highness Prince Al-Majid Mandar Sultan Al-Fahd Al-Ahran – in his honourable position as Commander in Chief of Joint Saudi Arabian Forces – made his distinguished presence known yesterday at RSAF, Jeddah. He was greeted by Air Commodore Abdullah Rajab Al-Misrah and introduced to the American direction of personnel operations, Tom Adams..." blah blah...

I remembered my unfavourable impressions of Adams after a confrontational encounter with the unpleasant tyrant. I knew that he had spent far too long spraying napalm on the Mekong Delta to remain a human being. "Could I have the key to Mr.Shelley's office?" I asked Adams on the morning of my lesson observation. Shelley was an idle British Director of Studies who did nothing all day. I didn't like him but I needed the key to his office so I could look at my papers. Adams looked strangely at me. Maybe he thought I was an old hippy or else perhaps a new hyper? Whatever.. Shelley suddenly appeared and then there was an order to appear in the Air Commodore's office at once.

"Don't you EVER speak to me like that again!" he bellowed.

"Are you doing a Coysh re-run, Commodore?" I asked out of context as I thought of the Dottore di Musica yelling at the unfortunate John Quinn in the SLS days. People could get ridiculously aggressive for no apparent reason and being in KSA didn't help. Stress management meant yelling at the fool in front of you - hopeless stuff.

"WHAT? Look, what Shelley does is his business and nothing to do with you!"

"So you think I was reporting Shelley for dereliction of duty?" I asked incredulously.

"Nonsense."

"I don't like your attitude."

"And I don't like yours."

"Git back to work, boy, " Adams roared."

"Fuck off!"

It was amazing to experience such unmitigated crap but that was RSAF. The worst aspects of the American Way were on daily display. Others drank their way through. Dan drank flash as if he was determined to destroy himself. Often he would collapse dead drunk or else strip naked and pee over the dead cacti outside his concrete bungalow. Despite his binges he always seemed to manage to get to work

"Jimmy Beam been a long time gone" he muttered endlessly as he pulled on his thirtieth cigarette of the morning. I found all this quite intolerable. I had phoned my wife but I knew that my marriage was over. She had money so she didn't need my morose emotional dependency now that our son was growing up. She announced that she was going to be an independent single parent while I was going to lose everything like all Western men who suffered under the scourge of feminism. None of the Saudis would have put up with a minute of her rejection speech

"I'm not interested in your problems any more. It's over!" she spat from thousands of miles away. I felt like dying. What about my wonderful son whom I loved to distraction? Would I ever see him again? Harbouring such thoughts I languished helplessly for weeks till eventually I was able to turn my back on RSAF Jeddah. I could forget about religious police, morals police, security police, expat Thatcherites and all the rest of the shite that made up life in the Lockheed horror show. Here today, gone tomorrow and return to UKAY to get divorced then commit suicide. One contract after another, from job to job, a way of existence confirming my father's words that I couldn't stick at anything. The only thing was that there didn't seem anything worth sticking to.

I was now in Qatar on a temporary British Council contract. I was stuck in a flat near Doha International Airport sometime in 1987. I was working as a hack English instructor for the Qatari Petroleum Company (QGPC). The training department was run by pompous characters who looked down on teachers when they were teachers themselves. An Eric Burden General Norriega pineapple face lookalike was the main man. This creep had become a Bahai so his vows of truth gave him a superior air to the moronic teachers suffering under his yoke. Besides being a creep he was also a self-important traitor to all things Western. He made it clear that he hated teachers and allocated me and my two colleagues trivial and mind-deadening tasks.

"Go to the language lab and fill in the answers to the tape on the Direct English Data Bank," he ordered. His Newcastle grind was annoying as he spewed out his mangled vowels.

At the Data Bank I messed up the dialogues.

"Have you seen Ahmed today? – Mind your own business

"Did you drink coffee? – No I got smashed on whisky"

"What's your name? – Eh?"

" Would you open the door, please? – Up you pal"

etc.

Similarly childish responses were recorded for future students. I calculated that I would be long gone before anybody got round to using the material. What did Pineapple expect from British Council contractors who were just in for a fast buck? Surely he didn't expect a commitment to the empty existence of Qatar? Revenge came on the last day.

"We'll meet at three o'clock to discuss your Progress Report," he stated flatly.

But the teachers had already been paid two days before departure. Flight arrangements had been made with Gulf Air to fly out mid-morning. Students had agreed to drive the stupid chalkies to the airport. At 10 a.m.

sharp a convoy of vehicles moved towards the exit of QGPC. Pineapple stood with a shocked expression as we waved a jeering goodbye. Thus another successful escape was carried out for the usual entirely inadequate financial returns. Teachers weren't destined to get rich or famous. They were like the stereotypes in the textbooks, poor and unknown.

..........................................................................................

# CAIRO AND MORE OF THE SAME

An opportunity came to work with Snamprogetti, an offshoot of AGIP, the Italian oil company. Dr. Terence Coysh of SLS vintage just happened to be doing the interviewing. At the shoddy agent's office off Regent Street there was the Dottore, smart in expensive Italian suit and looking as Italian as an Italian. I was told right away that I had the job since Terence had recognized me from the wonderful days back in Dhahran. So I flew out to Cairo where a wastaman was waiting at the airport to guide me through customs, always an invaluable help in difficult countries. A car drove me straight away to quite a reasonable hotel somewhere in the Dohi area. For three weeks Terence and I pretended to be important training consultants while we took advantage of the free food and accommodation. Work was at a squalid depot on the outskirts of the city. Hours were an easy nine to three, five days a week. We had to motivate a bunch of intelligent and pleasant Egyptian engineers, including one woman who was culturally conditioned to say nothing. Although she was clearly very capable, a male member of the class always spoke for her. Underneath all the gloss it was just the same old Tefling merry-go-round although we were pleasantly surprised to be handed out wads of local currency as spending money. Then we left the hotel to be put up in a large house in Mohandessin where we had a personal driver and manservant who did everything for nothing a week. Dottore Coysh had a terrible attitude towards the manservant – I was very shocked one day to listen to his rude manner after the poor guy had failed to iron a shirt to the high standards of the ex-opera singer. No wonder the infidels were heartily disliked with this sort of ignorance in play. The contrast between the conditions of foreigners and the wretched natives was astonishing. Bruno Vantini the depressed Italian Training Manager openly despised Egyptians, discussed opera in great detail with his wife and the Dottore while he piled up the money. Working for AGIP wasn't so bad with 2000 Egyptian pounds to spend locally plus sterling pounds salary paid outside the country. It was a better deal than many others although there were drawbacks. We found it necessary to dine in style at upmarket international hotels to avoid being poisoned by the local food. This wasn't prejudice against Egyptian cuisine but more of an illustration that all the good locally produced meat and vegetables were exported abroad. Colonialism never ceased. After work we could look round the Hanghalili souk in central Cairo, wasting money on various trinkets while the average Gyppo survived on 120 EP per month. We saw the pyramids of course and each afternoon we were served afternoon tea in the old colonial style at the Gizira Club. It was all very pleasant. I admired the new leather jacket I had bought. I felt well off being able to afford to travel first class on the train to Alexandria. There were unbearably hot weekends at Port Said on the Red Sea. Out of politeness to the families who had invited us I spent five or six hours baking under a canopy on a beach in boiling heat, unwillingly eating the hard-boiled eggs on offer. I disliked eggs but didn't want to appear rude The biggest bonus was the unexpected free telephone line to the world. For some reason I was able to make international calls and calculated that I would be far away when the huge bill came in for the long conversations to the USA and Europe. But I hadn't quite escaped domestic problems back in the UK – an unexpected week's leave in the middle of the contract made a big hole in the salary but even so Cairo had been OK. Naturally I was forced into an unwilling state of chastity since there had been nothing on offer save frightful-looking harridans who made crude offers in the street. Only a suicide would have taken up such invitations to die. The visiting Saudis seemed to have no such qualms as they enjoyed the weak Gyppo beer while discussing terms with filthy harlots of the lowest type. The Saudis weren't famous for their powers of imagination. I couldn't really relate to a culture that officially denied free sexual relations. Heavy-duty influences seemed to inhibit normal emotional development and anyway the strictures of Islam discouraged girlfriends in the Western fashion. It was plain depressing to see men kissing and walking down the street holding hands. I didn't identify with the boys who took a shine to each other or else found solace with women of the paying variety. All the things that were pleasurable in life appeared to meet with disapproval in places under religious influence. Maybe things were a bit freer in Syria or the Emirates but any 1960s libertarian like myself found the Arab straight street hard going. I got to a stage of resigned indifference to the general hypocrisy but the Calvinist in me kept me coming back for more punishment. I watched women unveiling once they'd got on a plane out of the country, lighting up cigarettes and downing the alcohol. None of it made sense except that it was oil that made the world go round and I was working for an oil company. However I was still a poor teacher. Have you ever met a rich teacher?

The classic STREAMLINE series illustrates the point well.

"Is Mr.Wilson a teacher? Yes he is."

"Does he live in a small house? Yes he does."

"Is he poor? Yes he is."

"Why is he a teacher? Ask Mr.Wilson."

The cartoon pictures of Mr.Wilson bring to mind some small northern town suburban nightmare in a 1962 England. He looks shoddy and down-trodden while he drives a battered Morris Minor. His life of emptiness brings tears to your eyes.

The years of teaching this dreadful book had fused my mental equipment. I was suffering from STREAMLINE DEPARTURES, STREAMLINE CONNECTIONS AND STREAMLINE DESTINATIONS. The drivel ran around my brain like a disease. There was no cure since the TEFL plague had spread round the world. The authors of STREAMLINE must have made a fortune and retired long ago. I wasn't collecting the royalties though and as a carrier of the TEFL virus I was always liable to be called back to some impossible situation. Circumstances took me back to the JAM. Dan Breem from the Lockheed days gave me a call. I was surprised to hear that he was still alive.

"I've got a prostitute lined up for you. All you have to do is get down to Coventry and you'll be in the JAM within a few days."

Dan coughed up his lungs as he gave me the details. I got down there after becoming bored with my solitary confinement in the north of Scotland. At the agent's office in Coventry Dan was waiting looking like Death warmed up. He was on a bender. Along with brand new colleagues, we made our way to the Excelsior Hotel at Gatwick. We were being put up there at company expense for a two-day briefing. This was the usual softening up process although this outfit were certainly generous with travelling expenses. They didn't turn a hair as I presented a claim for hundreds of pounds.

"Just order what you want," said the flashy agent producing a gold Amex card. The atmosphere was late 1988 with the possibility of a property crash looming in the UK. Dan obviously didn't care as he hit the bottle for free. After the freebie the chalkies flew to Malta. There it was the predictable scenario of being taken care of by Stavalos and his moneymaking

Mafioso. Dan though didn't see much as he was paralytic on arrival and had to be put to bed. Next morning at 11 a.m I was astonished to see Dan at the bar downing his fifth beer. At lunch he stumbled over out of his brains, knocking over tables and muttering nonsense to the diners. Then the taxi came to take us contractors to the airport. The depressing scene presented itself with shouting Libyans crowding the check-in as if the word "queue" didn't exist. You were back in the JAM right enough. You had to keep your feelings to yourself and not lash out at the first Libyan who tried to skip the queue. Wait for your revenge, pal, I muttered under my breath. Meanwhile Dan was still drinking, even on the short flight from Malta to Tripoli. When the plane landed he fell off the plane, dropped his passport at immigration control before crashing senseless on the ground. Apathetic security police arrested the mad Irishman and locked him in a cupboard. Eventually he was released and joined the rest of us on the drive to Misrata where we were working for Kobe Steel, Japan. Hours later after a long drive along the coast we reached the compound.

"I'm the Chief Instructor," said a rough Glaswegian accent." What I say goes."

Inside his portakabin bottles were everywhere. "Are ye drinking?" he asked. Dan at once took up the offer while the rest of the new arrivals politely declined. What was this scene? It transpired that Alistair McDoom had gone crazy. He'd gone on a bender after assaulting a Libyan student. He was now under house arrest before being taken back to be sectioned in the UK. McDoom had no idea that he was teaching uneducated peasant farmers. He'd assumed that he was teaching academics who had been drafted in to operate an advanced steel production plant. He had been totally unable to communicate with his students and one day he had lost his cool with negative results. He was lucky not to be sent to jail immediately – another nutter trying to find a place between theory and practice.

The teaching started. It was horrendous. There were no books for the first two weeks, which meant adlibbing six hours a day, six days a week. There were twenty students crammed into the classroom. They listened expectantly as I danced up and down like a lunatic. Such an exercise would break many people who imagine that "teaching" only means standing in front of people telling them what to do. McDoom followed this notion.

"Ahm telting your whit tae dae" he shouted in futility. "Ahs larnin yous the Glesca, savvy?" The students stared blankly at the mental patient from Jockland.

The McDoom pedagogical method was followed by others such as the new Fire Safety Officer. This man had nil teaching experience and was burdened by an impossibly broad Geordie accent. I could never understand why people seemed quite incapable of changing their accent and pronunciation or recognizing that they were talking to foreigners in what was to them a foreign language.

"Right you lot. I'm the new Fire Safety Officer," shouted the new Fire Safety Officer. He shouted as he wrote stuff on the board while ordering confused students to copy it all down. No wonder the steel plant failed to function properly.

I couldn't sleep. The full horror of being back in the JAM was almost too much to endure. I was also deeply worried about an impending housing crash. I was highly indebted to Barclays Bank, interest rates were increasing and my financial fortunes were taking a marked turn for the very worst. My life seemed to have gone nowhere at all despite all my efforts. The priggish Austrian doctor gave me a disapproving look when I asked for some good sleeping pills. With a bad grace he signed the prescription allowing me some chemical relief. Eventually I made excuses, changed the contract so that I could exit sooner rather than later. The only benefit from this trip was seeing Leptis Magna again – the old Roman city was as wonderful as ever. Its perfectly preserved buildings ignored the piles of rubbish piled up beside the roadside. A few dead goats wouldn't make much difference to the past glories of the Roman Empire. Things hadn't really changed here since 200 AD.

I asked myself when all these Middle East trips were going to end? It wasn't a life doing contracts in dustbowls, staying for a while, then doing a runner back to the UK and endless and pointless supply work. The unsatisfactory lifestyle seemed to go on forever. There was no end in sight as the property crash of 1989 condemned me and millions of others to continuing penury. We were all fools who had believed in the so-called property-owning democracy. I struggled on with the supply until the local management of schools initiative kyboshed my unambitious meanderings. I was without a proper career but there was always a job in the JAM when things got desperate.

"No. Not the JAM again!" I said to myself. I'd sent my CV off to an outfit called AFMEMCO that had offered me a job over the phone at tragic rates of pay. I met a character called Tellessey at Gatwick airport, gratefully accepted his free coffee and flew off to Malta. The contract stated nine weeks work, three weeks holiday, free "board and lodging" and a dismal salary of £1200 per month, much less than I'd been getting in Cairo. I was further appalled by the draconian work schedule that meant slaving for 11 hours a day for sixty-three days in a row. Barclays Bank were on my tail though, my overdraft was rising by the hour so as an ex-poshboy from Glasgow I had to bite the bullet. This was part of the continuing story of Decline and Fall. I was falling while Department of Trade licences were being granted to foreign charlatans like Tellessey. He could make money out of the over-educated mugs of the Western world while I could only bemoan my hopeless financial situation.

At the dreadful Tripoli International Airport it was a familiar scene – tired revolutionary slogans still adorning the airport but these days there was only apathy. Nobody was chanting ARABYA JAMAHARIYA any more. Libya was in bits like me.

"This visa no good," snarled the passport chappie. "You go back Malta"

"But it's a perfectly valid business visa."

"This cost $500."

"But I'm working for the Sirte Oil Company. I don't need to pay anything."

"You go back Malta."

"No I'm staying."

Questions arose in my mind. Why was I staying? How could I avoid yet another masochistic torture session? But there wasn't much at home – only sporadic supply work and a mountain of debt. I gritted my teeth. I thought of the awful nine weeks ahead, the dismal accommodation, the unspeakable food and of course the unspeakable work. By now the passport chappie had given up trying to make me change $500 in worthless dinars at the official rate of exchange. I wasn't going to be conned into throwing my money away. I walked out into the arrivals hall but there was nobody there to meet me despite Tellessey's assurance that a car would be laid on. I hailed a taxi, telling the driver to take me to the Sirte "guest-house". There nobody had heard of me but nevertheless I was given a room. Next day I spoke to the Head of the English Department at Sirte, a character called Mike Sly. He sounded entirely indifferent to the mad tale of yet another Tefler down on his luck. I flew up to Marsa el Brega with a sinking heart. I got off the plane to see close at hand the grim sight of an oil and gas plant. I also saw Mike Sly waiting for me. He was an obvious alcoholic with years of debauchery all over his prematurely lined face. He drove me to my " accommodation".

"I'm just here for the night, presumably" I asked knowing that the answer would be unfavourable. "I was promised a flat, not a portakabin."

"No these are your quarters. You'll love them " sneered Sly.

Inside my quarters the walls were a shit brown with the most basic of furniture. This was true dosshouse living. I had been wise to bring along some of Charles Bukowski's best sellers for bedtime reading. I would have plenty of miserable nights to pass all alone with only Henry Chianski for company. Bukowski knew the score.

At Sirte I was to experience baptism by fire. Paul Rutherford, ex-British Aerospace Brummie jeered.

"Another contractor!" he scoffed. Sitting in the office were other characters, also it turned out on the lousy AFMEMCO contract. Crowe was a rebel as he had put up a Trade Union sign.

"It's awful, isn't it?"

"Yes. Awful." I agreed as I sank into depression. I was going mad with worry as I had foolishly installed some Nigerians in my London flat. Their first cheque had bounced, they weren't paying the rent and I didn't have an agent to manage the property. It was a bad omen. I wasn't to know that the rent would never be paid or that I would come back to a wrecked flat that would cost thousands to repair. And just as well too or I would not survived stuck my barrel of curses. Communication from Libya was difficult, there was no e-mail and the telephone system was unreliable. How was I going to endure the next few months all for a miserly nothing at all a month? Next-door Mike Sly made it plain that he couldn't care less. Why should he on his £36000 a year tax-free, ten years in the job and as much drink and dope as he could lay his hands on? The attitude of long term Sirte teachers was similarly hostile and contemptuous. They'd been rotting for years in self-importance and conceit and weren't used to new faces. They enjoyed higher salaries than the AFMEMCO contractors. So the horrendous days crawled past, an insult to mind and body. The call of the mosque went at 5 a.m. as I dragged myself out of bed.

ALLAH ALLAH ALLAHAHKBAR.. The racket drilled into the internal recesses of my crushed consciousness. The wasted years in education hammered home the message that this was the price to be paid for non-conformity. Why hadn't I been an accountant? The moon was still shining in the sky as a lone figure made its way to the disgusting mess hall. The prospect of seeing sneering Libyans first thing in the morning was not appealing but it was either eat or starve. The bus came to pick up the students and staff alike. The noise, sweat and general mayhem represented three sound reasons for resigning immediately. The miserably long hours were absolutely killing. How was it that sharpsters like Tellessey were getting rich while disillusioned idealists from the European and American 1960s were reading Bukowski in the JAM?

The AFMEMCO contractors were an odd bunch. They were either too young or straight or sullen, nasty bastards like Andrew, an old cowboy soak with boots and a high self-regard. Hillman was 35 from Dagenham but he didn't like to admit it. He was a brilliant linguist but his personality was deeply hidden – he tried to be as Arab as possible. I was

109. Being with people I didn't want to be with made every day a torture beyond description. The hell that was other people was alive and well but I was fading away. All things come to an end though and I resigned. Surely supply was better than this bucket of shit? Or was it?

Back in Scotland the call to the JAM came yet AGAIN! Sirte Oil Company had decided on direct hire and my name was on the list of hirelings. Several months later I found myself back in the lavatory I had just left. This time round I was a real Sirte man on thirty five days work plus twenty one days paid leave. It was still portakabin living as silent men in silent rooms contemplated why they had gone wrong. Mr. Perfect Steve Cotton sat hunched over his typewriter producing endless tests to keep the bonkers Training Center open. Julian Rich remembered South Africa as he studiously ignored everybody. His face only lit up when he spoke on the phone to some lady friend.

"Thanks so much for a wonderful time" he enthused in a strong Voertrekker accent.

Mike Sly was now demoted after being drunk and stoned once too often. This was a good move for him – same salary, no responsibility. Muktar a Libyan took over as Head of Department, thus guaranteeing even more inefficiency and disorganization. Professor Sly sat smoking one roll –up after another, saying nothing, his bloodshot eyes rolling round in their sockets. His faithless wife had just left him so he was now alone to reflect on his useless life. He dreamed of Brighton as he delivered another terrible Kernel lesson.

Steve Neill had done ten years and looked it. He talked like a proselytising convert.

"What about British society? Criticizing Gadaffi is all very well. Lockerbie is just an excuse for the Americans to put pressure on Libya and cause an internal insurrection." He gasped over his sixtieth cancer tube of the day. Steve liked to assume inside political knowledge and was happy to have it known that he had influence where it counted. Once when he and several others were going on leave they had been stranded at the Tripoli docks for five days without tickets or accommodation. Steve had finally made a desperate call to the big boss Mr.Bennayran who had ordered his minions to get things sorted out. This was a small triumph but Gadaffi continued to thrive regardless of the nightly discussions in the mess hall. Gadaffi was the kabir modir(big bossman)

"Your Gentlemen's Club " jeered Paul Rutherford contemptuously at the talkers as he walked off with his squash racket under his arm.

What a scene! Wooden lessons went on and on till at last the thirty-five days were over and I could escape for twenty-one days of freedom.

Now that air sanctions were in force the main routes out of the country were either by a vile journey by ferry to Malta or else by bus to Djerba in Tunisia, then on to Tunis for a flight to Amsterdam. I remembered the first journey out of the JAM when passengers had gone from Ras Lanuf on a Russian hydrofoil. The Med can be rough at any time of the year but with typical Libyan lack of foresight it hadn't been considered that the craft was entirely unsuitable for a long sea voyage. A few hours out from Ras Lanuf the engines stopped as the hydrofoil bucked and heaved in a heavy swell. Everybody was seasick. The craft stank of vomit, urine and shit. It was impossible to sit down, impossible to stand up and impossible to lie down without being thrown all over the place. Death didn't come this time and the Russian –owned heap of scrap limped into Valetta harbour to deposit its exhausted passengers like sacks of old turd. That was often the way in the Arab world – treated like rubbish and expected to obey orders without question. This was the post-colonial legacy, the formerly oppressed getting their own back on the white boys.

Arriving in Amsterdam was like entry to Paradise after the privations of Libya. At the 5 star hotel near Schipol the TV was showing soft porn. I had escaped from SPLAJ once again. In my imagination voices were screaming in madness but now I could relax. I was back in the Western sphere, no longer responsible for the problems produced by American imperialism and not required to have meaningless and one-sided discussions on international affairs. Most of the time I had no opinions about anything or interest in anything save my own well being. I had nothing left to give to the waiting armies of potential English language students. I hated the whole thing – the high-earning roughie toughies who loathed teachers, the stereotyped small investors, the hard-drinking cowboys, the one-sided contracts and the authoritarian atmosphere that reduced sensitive, supposedly intelligent people to anguished hulks.

"How is everything? How are you? How is the President?" There wasn't much to say in response to such questions as you stood in front of the photocopier gobbling up trees. You weren't a human being but a goon who had taken "Education" too seriously while not realizing that smart operators ran the world. I told myself that money definitely mattered while intellectual insights and mushy ideals were on the sidelines. It was difficult to change the thinking of a lifetime that had got me absolutely nowhere. At least now I was in Amsterdam. I lit up a joint and reflected on my melancholy tale.

I did a few trips back and forward to Libya till inevitably I got bored with all of it. Rather than get my finances in order I didn't return after going on leave. I thought that I would get my life together instead but poor boys aren't allowed to do that. They have to keep working. Work back in Scotland dried up after I'd walked out of the school in Fraserburgh. I felt then that I was completely finished as a teacher. It was the summer with nothing on offer save another contract in the JAM organized by the SLS criminals who had landed me up shit creek back in Dhahran. This job turned out to one of the worst ones of all. Maybe it was because I was burned-out and couldn't hack it any more. Months of delays and wind-ups eventually produced a flight to Malta then a miserable journey on a dirty old steamer to the dismal Tripoli. At the disaster of a port mad crowds pushed and shoved their way through tiny passages. Aggressive customs officials unceremoniously opened luggage and rifled rudely through their contents. Then I was out into the dust on my way up to the RASCO compound at Ras Lanuf., the desert nowhere 700 km up from Tripoli. Here I felt that life was too short to waste by working in such places. I hated the two young teachers on sight. Mike Tarkony was a ghastly precocious fellow of 29 with a self-righteous and patronizing air. Clearly he disapproved of anybody unlike himself or older. Tim Quinn wasn't quite so bad but he was hard as nails and psychologically empty in a way that only an upbringing on an RAF base in Cyprus could produce.

"Wake me up so that I can tell you that you're a cunt" was his idea of humour.

Then there was John Baines, a silent chap from Manchester who said nothing for weeks. If Hell had a name then for me it would be Ras Lanuf.

News from the JAM was that a burned-out teacher yells from Hell that it's all over with the teaching bullshit. Chalky dogsbody resigns from bum job in the desert. Reason – psychological instability. The guy's flakey men. He needs 25mg of Phrenegen to sleep away the memories of his rotten woman.

I spent my time making calculations. I was having problems with my lady friend, a Deutsche Angstfrau who seemed to me to be selfish, conceited and a real money bitch. She had no understanding of the problems faced by a broke teacher from the UK. As the bus packed with wage slaves rolled over the desert I despaired of my very existence. I couldn't understand why I put myself through such troughs of negativity and futility. I was unable to explain to the hard cow that I was experiencing daily crucifixion in the name of the moneylenders. I heard her voice on the phone – self-confident and organized in the manner of the financially secure. Maybe it was her use of the English language but I couldn't identify with her statements. "I'm making my plans till December. I'm with Britt, Jorg and Uwe, going to Hamburg to stay in Karin's flat, then on to Wiesbaden to see Bettina. Next Munchen then Nizza"

Very nice for some people I lamented. She didn't care about me. This was a woman who had made out that she was short of money. I was in paroxysms of Angst to have fallen for such a cuntess. Being in love with this middle-aged man-eater was a heavy scene, all bucks and fucks stuff. I hated myself for behaving like a lovesick madman but she'd got under my skin. I bleated out my love for her as I suffered in the Ras Lanuf slave labour camp. My lessons were rubbish and every day was identical – out on to the Soweto-style street at 5.30 a.m., sloppy breakfast in the huge mess hall, a dismal journey on a crappy bus to the Training Center and not a woman in sight. I was lucky to get there at all as the driver drove like a maniac. The other passengers gave off an air of downbeat depression. As the days of suffering went past I told myself that I had to deal with my many creditors but it all became too much. I handed in my resignation. The crackpot relationship with the German was destroying me as I thought that I was passionately "in love" for the first time in my life. This was the same as being mentally ill.

I wrote to the Angstfrau.

"If you think you are mentally ill then just consider my schizophrenic sensitivities," said my letter. I saw myself taking myself apart as I committed my damnation epitaph to paper. Uncontrollable emotions tore me apart dragging me into a purgatorial and bottomless abyss .I had only the bitch's voice on the phone once a week to give me crumbs of comfort. I phoned her in Deutschland but she wasn't there.

"Have a good time down there," said her son's voice meaninglessly form Hamburg. How could Jorg even begin to understand my abysmal situation in Libya? The voices continued inside my flawed brain. I cursed the Angstfrau as a megalomaniac, immature, a crass materialist and enemy of men. After yet another awful day at the Training Center I walked along the beach feeling my stomach protest at my production line dinner. I was having a nervous breakdown. I felt as devastated as 1945 Berlin as I languished in darkest sorrow. Her brassy voice came over from Wiesbaden. Apparently she had been out dancing all night with her tearaway 30-year-old daughter. I deeply resented her oldest swinger in town outlook while I was in the middle of losing all control over my memories, dreams and reflections. In the bus my twisted perspective produced an imperialist picture of gooks looking out dumbly at the Dantean landscape. Miserable Iraqis gabbled in incomprehensible lingo. I felt like the last of the Empire Loyalists as I failed to come to terms with my Taureg compatriots. I had been born anachronistically after 1945 and now had sentenced myself to personal destruction in the training centres of the world. I had nobody to talk to as I bottled up my rage and frustration. I envisaged arriving in

Nizza in a towering fury, smashing her car before destroying all the possessions she loved so much. I saw myself leaving her battered and bruised before committing hari-kari in a blaze of romantic glory. The Angstfrau's malefic spirit had reduced me to the role of a whingeing dog. I could just see the headlines in the "Guardian".

MAD CHALKIE FROM JOCKLAND COMMITS SUICIDE AFTER ASSAULTING SEPARATED LOLITA WIFE OF LEADING KIEL BUSINESSMAN

I vowed never to repeat this experience. I was living a life for madmen only even if I still couldn't understand why I had repeated the exercise in self-mortification on so many occasions. I knew I was pursuing chimera in the form of a woman who admitted to having no conscience. I was a fool earning paltry sums in order to stay barely solvent in the doomed UK. I was without purpose or direction in the insanity of the military-industrial-complex. As an industrial nobody myself, I was paying a dire penalty for failure to belong and conform to the consumer ethos. I looked at my ghastly colleagues, thinking that abandoning ship, dereliction of duty and refusal to obey orders were noble concepts indeed. I sat in the staff room whiling away the vacuous hours. Why was I an Earthling anyway and why was I on the planet? Each day felt like a year. I was middle-aged unemployable Britisher, a 1960s drop out, stung by the 1989 property crash. Everything was awful. The students seemed aggressive and demanding. Grammar lawyers asked obscure questions about irrelevant details. They appeared like wild animals as I wrote out my lines for the sale of Lithium and other major tranquillizers. With dead souls for company doing solitary in the JAM there seemed no hope at all. It didn't seem likely that I would rise from the ashes of my own funeral pyre as I reached bottom surrounded by the spiritual corpse of the classless society. I felt like the old washout of the sand totally at odds with urban streetcred. As I ate my slops in the gasworks canteen I dreamed of good meals and getting out of the fucking country. I heard the bus driver say "Halas-O" for the last time. Then supervisor Othman came to take me to the airport. As the plane took off for Tripoli I knew that I was seeing Ras Lanuf for the last time. That loser's gulag wouldn't see me again. I had been paid by the SLS robbers to rot in a land of the dead, a sad saga of life among remnants and cast-offs. As the plane touched down at Nizza I knew I was back in the clutches of the Angstfrau and so-called "civilization". Was there any truth in the Nietzschean imperative of adversity killing you or making you stronger? As I was still alive I would no doubt find out.

.........................................................................................

# ENDLESS PRESSURE AND LIFE UNDER THE SYSTEM

Back in the Shabbah apartments outside Kuwait City I marvelled at my all-round incompetence. Now I was writing out some bleak memoirs showing how easy it was to get fired from turdheaps. Who wanted to actually work for a living? I cursed my failure to become a famous film star. I had foolishly thought in the past that I would find fulfilment in career mysticism but SATORI hadn't come up with anything worthwhile save the idea that I hated the world in which I found myself. I naturally only had myself to blame. Auditory hallucinations occupied my waking hours as I stared at the walls of the Kuwait box in the sky.

"You'll regret it. Nobody will want to know you. All your friends will be doing well. This easy osey hippy happy attitude will get you nowhere." My father had of course been absolutely right way back in the 60s. I had got absolutely nowhere. I wasn't interested in anything save having a comfortable life preferably financed by some generous benefactor with a large bank account. I dreamed of rich widows handing out wads of cash to slothful Lotharios round the universe. It was time that the women paid up,

"What are you interested in?" the Angstfrau had asked.

"The ESOTERIC".

But she hadn't understood what I was saying which was hardly surprising. I was on a road that required total disengagement from the enormous bore of being a company man, doing what you were told and fitting in with gays and political correctness. I was an out of style male with the usual masculine emotional needs. It was just that communication with a ball-breaker like the Angstfrau required convoluted explanations. She was probably too old for me as her understanding of the "esoteric" and mine were rather different. Certainly she was "artistic" with deep emotional sensitivities but she didn't have to earn her living, a pleasant state of affairs that naturally encouraged the development of cultural taste and sophistication. The essential point was that she wasn't a teacher. She was a German woman who had married young and was accustomed to being kept in style by her rich businessman husband. I couldn't compete at the end of the day.

I had failed to shine in the universal competition, having done little or nothing to promote myself. I'd opted for the narrowest of options instead of saying no to teaching. As a result of my earlier decisions in life I was now mouldering away in the Sabeh-al Salem area of Kuwait City listening to the endless roar of traffic on the nearby superhighway. In front of me was the dreadful American DLI manual Book 19. This was the stalwart teaching aid that would put a few more nails in my personal coffin. If this was the only focus I thought then I might as well self-terminate immediately. It was a familiar scene with me alone with myself in a room. The tape in my head whizzed over past events and experiences, some good, most appalling. When you are out on a limb you know there is no going back to lost halcyon days. Life was a rollercoaster with your destiny firmly mapped out to bring your remains crashing down in ruins.

"You must arrange yourself with this world, otherwise nothing will be right" preached the Angstfrau from her position of leisured ease. I knew there was no possibility of unlocking the tape, which was stuck in 1963. I had accepted nothing at all about the institutional pantomime. I failed to see why I should have to accept patronizing lectures from a mercenary who had married purely for money. Stupidly I still believed in love. I read her letter stuck in the deserts of North Africa feeling as though I was on my last mission to disaster. Back here in Hawally I thought over the years of self-abnegation and endless humiliation in the service of worthless enterprises. I was astonished that I had allowed myself to be victimized by the dismally inferior standards emanating from the debased British educational system. That was the story of my life to date. I'd been taken in by myths, cretins and sewer rats whose only claim to fame was to be lavatory graduates from some downmarket technical college. The atmosphere in the 1960s had influenced me to such an extent that I had done my utmost to deny my intelligence and to appear opposed on principle to elitism and privilege. Now I wanted to fight back, contemptuous of jumped-up corporals who had assumed the airs and graces of authority. They were all over the place, these old brylcreem boys from the slums, hardly able to talk proper English let alone teach it. The blarney merchants were employing the posh boys in order to line their pockets. I objected to my downward mobility but what could I do?

Crushed faces sat in the staff room of the Ministry or Defence Language School. MINDEF was ghastly. In typical programmed American style the learning approach guaranteed brain death. The British wage slaves were token Americans pretending to be important cogs in a futile quest. The first Gulf War had left plenty of openings for Teflers but at derisory rates of pay. The general delusion in the smoke-filled staff room was that there was any future at all in the Tefling cosmos. Teachers talked shop as the weary hours of enslavement dragged by. As prisoners in Kuwait they imagined they were living the good life when in reality they were fading away behind breeze blocks in the sand. They stared blankly at the superhighway and the scraggy goats eating plastic bags on the rubbish heap opposite the apartment building. It was important for the poor boys to regard themselves as esteemed professors. I found all this just part of the general psychological torture of being on a hiding to nothing. On the way out to Kuwait we'd been put up at the Hilton in Bahrain before facing reality. I regretted having any involvement with the shady Institute for Private Education that was employing me after being recruited by Network Overseas in London. I had seen it all before – incarceration under strip lighting and locked into featureless classrooms was all too familiar to a bitter teacher. I longed for the elusive Dolce Vita but for the foreseeable future I would only experience bitterness like Yasser Arafat. Unlike the sadly deceased PLO property magnate I didn't have any machine guns or mean to use them. I did however harbour the sincere intention to drop the dustbowl scene forever. Despite all my efforts to stay afloat financially my position was dire and I was facing bankruptcy.

Even so I could see that my last runner was close at hand. Later I was informed that my departure from Kuwait was "highly irregular".

"Are you sincere in your intention?" had been a key question back in the Exegesis seminar days. I hadn't had the slightest understanding of sincerity at the time but now immersed in the Tefling dungheap I knew that commitment to my own salvation was of crucial importance. Shabby old Teflers had apparently lost any capacity for inner development. Instead they postured as upholders of a dubious government morality rather than dismiss the social control nonsense out of hand. Like me they needed the money. I came back to my cell in the apartment tower block feeling frustrated and disgusted with all and sundry. With a deep hatred I thought of language labs, computers, TEFL libraries, staff meetings, classrooms and all the rest. I reserved a particular venom for the founder of TEFL whoever that might be. I dreamed of abolishing the British Council and firing the pretentious fools who thought that the British way of life was the best in the world. I found that there was something especially offensive about Council types. They were senior prefect characters who were inspired by a boundless enthusiasm for Tefling, Queen and country, Shakespeare and literary criticism. These bums saw themselves as superior public school beings in the low world of linguistic bullshit. Naturally they spoke five languages fluently and identified totally with the Organization's viewpoint. The British Council in my opinion represented the worst aspects of intellectual snobbery, low pay and emotional vacuity. Unpleasant examples of Britain's worst people shouted out of the smutty pages of dull academic journals. I saw puerile papers being delivered by pompous pedagogues with Alzheimer's. The subject matter was quite meaningless on the level of: trivial questions and answers.

"Is John a man?" "Yes he is."

"Is Mary a woman?" "No she isn't."

Somehow such absurdities passed as serious topics worthy of discussion. I was losing any perspective in my misguided attempts to redress the balance in favour of the practical use of language The trouble was that cost-effectiveness and management speak had spread round the world. No job was secure as the time and motion people justified mass sackings under the glorious banner of Organization and Methods. "Quality management" tore apart what was left of civilized social relations as the clones at HQ churned out seas of statistics. I looked back at the pointless years in the SYSTEM. I had no interest in teaching anybody anything that advanced the creeping menace of crypto-fascism. I didn't see my role as that of a state policeman furthering the cause of a high surveillance society. I knew fine that if your face didn't fit then you had problems in the washed-up UK. I had had enough of its mad class system and psycho values. Basically, in my state of ultimate pessimism, I regarded everything as a major problem as the world appeared to be falling into terminal decline. MEIN GOTT GODDAM BRITISCHER CRAP!!"I'm a teeeaachaarrr!! I don't want to be a fucking teacher but I'm still a fucking teacher. I hate these jersey robots with their unstylish clothes, poofter demeanour and teeeaaachhharrr speak" The gibbering teacher was taken away by the men in white coats. It can happen to you.

..............................................................................

# LESSONS, DIALOGUES AND OTHER STUFF

No wonder that the teaching situation is regarded with disdain. Teachers get paid unprofessional salaries but are still expected to act "professionally".

Soon it will be like this. Crowds of lunatics with MA s and PhD s stand around schools round the world.

"Any supply work?"

"Three hours work at £5 per hour. But only if you are under 25."

Thousands of high IQ hands shoot into the air.

"ME, Sir. ME! ME!"

"And as for the rest of yous there's always International House round the corner at £3.50 per hour. Count yourselves lucky. Remember there's a turd-eating competition sponsored by the British Council. The teacher who manages to work for the largest number of un-accredited private language schools for the least amount of money will be presented with the COUNCIL TURD PRIZE. "

"Well taught" scowled Mr.Groveller the International House Gauleiter to Dr.Pure Hatred. "Yev got the shit-eating grin prize for selfless dedication to your self-destruction. Ya broke yer own heart and spirit and we're pleased here at IH that yev reduced yersels tae a physical wreck, ye ken. To show our appreciation here's a copy of the new IH Training Programme."

An excrement-covered copy of Streamline hit Mr.Groveller's empty skull. Sand poured out.

I wondered why people in the "profession" ended up in situations of utter humiliation. Were they so afraid of authority that they were terrified to have an opinion, let alone think about having one? Reliable troopers died quietly.

"Yes, Headmaster. No Headmistress. Whatever you think best, Head of Department. I quite agree with you, concerned parent. I really want to help, Minister."

With such snivelling and sycophantic attitudes it was unlikely that "respectable teachers" would have the slightest influence on the accountants at HQ. They were unwilling participants in dated managerial initiatives that might just have been relevant to General Motors in a 1964 Detroit. Whatever way you looked at it somebody was bound to be on your case.

"We've had a call from a concerned parent, Mr.Reslet."

"You were seen reading a book in class, Mr.Reslet."

"The Headmaster wants to see you immediately."

"Report to the Equal Opportunities Board tomorrow."

"I don't like your attitude."

"Watch your Ps and Qs Mr.Dullerson."

In Marsa el-Brega a teacher bored through yet another chapter of Streamline.He'd done 62 continuous days "teaching" and next day he was doing a runner.

"Is Mr.Wilson a teacher?"

"Yes he is."

"Is he poor?"

"Yes he is."

"Does he have a small car?"

"Yes he does."

"Is he a millionaire?"

"No he isn't"

The lessons dragged on minute by minute as the teacher kept looking at his watch. There were hours to go.

"Good answers, Ahmed, Nasser, Mohammed and Salem."

Inside the teacher's head his receptors were in a state of cosmic conflict. He wanted to scream and run back to the womb. But his mummy wasn't there and anyway he was in the JAM.

"Is Mr.Wilson a Muslim?"

"No he isn't."

"What does Islam mean?"

"Submission."

"Has Mr.Wilson submitted?"

"It certainly looks like it, folks."

"Is Mr.Wilson a masochist?"

"Indeed he is."

"Is Mrs.Wilson a schizophrenic?"

"Yes she's off her trolley."

This was the first class of the day he realized. He thought he'd done all his work till he remembered that he'd spent the previous night teaching in his dreams. He gritted his teeth as he tried to shut off his internal dialogue. As a talking machine he was expected to prompt the students towards the correct response. He had no choice save to externalise, forget his splitting headache and his painful stomach. Why couldn't he live a normal life like his mummy and daddy had taught him? He wanted to be a model 8-year-old boy once again, secure in the certainty that life was a great adventure.

"Now class there's a lot of homework to be done. I'd like you to do it for tomorrow."

"Yiz my teacher."

" I'll be awa' the morn" jeered the teacher from inside his brain.

"Well I'll see you tomorrow then. Enjoy your evening," he said pleasantly.

"Goodbye my teacher."

"Goodbye forever.."

"Yes class. Business is business and progress is progress. Write an essay on why teachers are not millionaires."

Jerusalem sighed as he sat down totally exhausted after yet another night on the eth.

"I've lost everything – repossessed – so I'm starting again," he muttered hopelessly.

At his 12th night party he had sung in a forthright fashion Blake's Hymn. Henceforth he was known as Jerusalem. Maybe that would be his funeral oration.

The Teflers gathered round to pay their last respects to Jerusalem, loyal to the very end.

"And did these feet in ancient time walk upon England's green and pleasant land" sang the Chief Instructor. "Fellow Teflers, Jerusalem was a Tefler to the last. He lived as he died writing his lesson plans. He was an example of all who follow Streamline. He was the true incarnation of Mr.Wilson, a superteacher who discussed grammar in his sleep. Only last night Jerusalem had been high on prepositions and the day before he had been mainlining phrasal verbs."

Piles of TEFL books were thrown on to the funeral pure as miles of tired print added fuel to the fire. Millions of bonkers Teflers shuffled round the globe as they faced their classes knowing that Jerusalem was no more.

The TEFL padre blessed the English language as he poured a bucket of sand on to the brainless deceased.

"Oh native speakers, foreign languages shall have no dominion. Chaucer guides our mission to those who spik no English. For the spirit of Mafeking shall triumph."

.................................................................................

# MR FLOP

Mr Flop wiz over the top. He wiz loopy man. He could hardly function any more, man. He'd been stuck in Straight Street for a thousand years. He was catatonic with the bore of Streamline. He wiz at the gates of Bedlam. He didnae ken any answers although he had no questions.

"Right class that's the end of the course. There's fuck all else to learn yous understand. If yous git tae the end of the book then yous can be sure of being sectioned. The Madness Academy is a highly selective skool. Only degenerate Streamliners can gain entrance..."

Mr.Flop chewed over his awful fate. He was sick of professionalism as he watched the precious moments of his life dribbling away on crowds of slow learners. His wooden lessons were legendary. He slumped on a chair feeling totally apathetic. He was close to being shipped out on a stretcher but he kept teaching. The writing was on the wall – he had reached his absolute limits regarding facing students and enduring solitude. He was getting too old and jaded to smile at all. Nobody spoke to him. He was alone with himself and a library of Streamline first editions. His life had been a failure – marriage, business, education. All his experience of absolutely everything had come to absolute ZERO. He would be sentenced to a CALL Centre (computer assisted learning) for the rest of his earthly existence. This was the fate of a Tefler flop like Mr.Flop who had spent many years contemplating the wasted years. He was pleased to know that somebody called Joe Dull had written a primer called the "WASTED YEARS". As a waster he would have to buy a copy. It appealed to Mr.Flop who had actually been to university. There he had studied a "somewhat vague discipline" called Sociology. He had been taught that he was a flop. He left university and became a teacher. Then he became a teacher and after that a Tefler. He hadn't found a better way of earning a living. He had made a mess of his finances; imprisoned by self-knowledge he knew that things always went wrong. He was an educational loser.

..........................................................................................

# NEW APPROACHES

"Line up you lot. I'm responsible for eliminating culture. You've dominated the language game for too long. Take out your PhD in Semiotics, that MA in Madness and Diploma in Dung. Light the fire will ya, Professor Chomsky? The names are helping these stakes to burn. I'm responsible for liberating the new business universities from wafflers and lectures on the iconography of neuro-linguistic programming."

To the sound of cheers buildings round the world emptied themselves of participle merchants, gerund dealers, semantic traders and epistemology brokers. At last it was over. The academic linguistic imperialists were being called to account for their effrontery in brainwashing a generation. It was clear that Education was a great lie designed by the good boys and girls who didn't want to leave the 6th form.

"Take those copulas, phonemes and fartones along with these Ethnomethodology textbooks along to the furnaces, men. Yer under arrest yous academics. You'll pay for malforming the perceptions of the Wilson years. Yous rewrote the reality script for the public schoolboys."

There were professors of bullshit here, literary critics underfoot and Chairmen of Sociology to the left of them.

"OK Laurie. You're first. If you're really doing Castaneda then you can jump into our specially prepared abyss. "

The Chairman expired as brilliant brains smashed in a world of inconceivable acts.

"Get a life. Get real. Get out of here!"

The bright boys got in touch with their emotions straight away.

"AAAAAAAAARRRRRRRRGGGGGGGGHHHHHHHHHHH-HHHH!"

The class bored on.

"John coulda gone to university but he didn't. He shoulda got a job instead. He oughta start work now." It was page 106 in the DLI.

"Good thinking" thought Mr.Flop as the endless and pointless hours dribbled past. If he'd gotta job then he wouldn't have had to teach the DLI. Thinking was a serious illness. Nobody wanted to think any more. Nobody wanted teachers or Mr.Grammar to tell them where it was at. The punters wanted something different surely?

**LOSER LESSONS IN POLITICAL INCORRECTNESS**

**Lessons went on round the world.**

**"Are you large?"**

**"Yes I am."**

**"Is he smaller than me?"**

**"Yes he is."**

**"What is the width of the room?"**

**"It is wide."**

**"Well how wide is the room?"**

**"It is 12m. width."**

**"Better. Good but not good enough."**

**"Yiz my teacharr."**

Read the following extract from the "Kelvinside Poshboy"( p.11) and answer the questions. The author is a product of the "Old School".

"Fred offered a prayer for Harold Wilson's new Labour government. It was 1964. Suddenly a chorus of mockery arose from the right-wingers from the veld. Their ribald jeers made it plain that they did not want Harold to win in Rhodesia. These stalwart Ian Smith fans would ensure that the Tiger Talks were doomed to failure. The Afrikaners shouted out their hatred of socialism to a man. Joe could see the faces of Pete Smithieman, Charles Court-Brown and Ronnie Reid bright red with rage. Fred stopped in mid-prayer and strongly rebuked the troublemakers. God apparently allowed all points of view with the natural exception of Marxism and Soviet Communism. Joe wondered in confusion if Harold Wilson's brand of PR was worth bothering about: all this stuff about the first hundred days and white-hot technological revolutions seemed facile and uninteresting. However all questions of significant issue were quickly relegated to yesterday's headlines as Joe became aware of Charles Court-Brown's extremely bad acne. His rapier intellect was of course quite out of Joe's league whose small brain was incapable of dealing with the highly erudite discussions on theological doctrine instigated by Fred the Leader. Fred had acne too so it didn't really matter what anybody was talking about. Despite being entirely unschooled in the rules of argument or debate Joe knew that spotty faces were a problem without a solution. Given this insight, Joe no reason to feel disadvantaged at not being able to string a sentence together. He saw no obligation to jump every time he heard the sound of a gerund of important-looking collective nouns being bandied about. This was the background to John Bunyan's weepy about life as struggle, the predecessor to the Mein Kampf best seller…."

1) Why do you think Fred offered a prayer for Harold Wilson's new Labour government?
2) Give reasons why Ian Smith was a much better prospect than the present upstart who is running Zimbabwe.
3) What is bad acne? Draw a picture illustrating your understanding of this condition.
4) Why were spotty faces a problem without solution?
5) Deconstruct the extract in terms of Afrikaner folklore.
6) Write an essay on the epistemology of life as struggle.
7) Describe Joe's attitude in ten sentences.
8) What on earth are significant issues?
9) Using appropriate theological references say why God allowed all points of view with the exception of Marxism and Soviet Communism.
10) Is the writer of this extract a mental patient or a teacher? Give reasons for your answer using Jungian archetypes as analytical structure.
11) Discuss the iconographic significance of prayer in the political process
12) Ask your analyst to give you a major tranquillizer.
13) Role play the extract in terms of the{ Rev.Blair.co.uk} phenomenon
14) Consider the place of the iambic tetrameter in government propaganda.
15) Write a defence of apartheid for the English Department at the University of Pietermaritzburg

Now that you have finished the course in Education for Losers, report to your local job club for advice on how to retrain as a graduate lavatory attendant. You also have great prospects as a shelf-stacker at minimum wage. You will need advice on writing a convincing CV so that your experience will help you obtain a suitable position. Refer to health and safety regulations that must be followed to the letter. Holding a mop and bucket requires skill and weeks of training on the job.

**AS IT REALLY IS ( a typical true story from the world of supply teaching)**

I went into the failing school on the Stonebridge Estate in North London. It was an early afternoon in 1988 . A crisis had arisen in a classroom with the teacher walking out in disgust. As a supply I was called in to deal with an untenable situation. I was greeted by louts sitting on the teacher's desk smoking cigarettes. As I ordered them to get back to their seats I was greeted by hostile shouts of "Fuck off". Threats were made that I would be beaten up. Somehow the "lesson" dragged on in an atmosphere of violence and intimidation. At the end of the day I went out to my car with a fellow teacher from New Zealand. A crowd of thugs was waiting for me. Pushing past the mob we got inside the vehicle. The thugs rocked the car from side to side making it impossible to drive off. Eventually we managed to get away but it had been a frightening experience. Next morning several louts who had been involved in the incident accosted me. They were furious that I had dared to confront them. I had given them the finger. They seemed to think that it was only them who had the right to use such gestures. I complained to the management but nothing happened. This was just another routine occurrence in the rough streets of the capital city. There were others too numerous to mention.

These days it is happening close to home. One evening in September I was walking down the streets of the town near where I lived .I was minding my own business as I made my way to my car. I noticed four youths on the other side of the street. I heard muttered curses and insults. "There's that fucker who works at the sports college. Fucking shit bag." I was furious at being subjected to this degrading treatment at the hands of people I didn't even know. Being very tall I stood out as an obvious target for abuse.

Suddenly some takeaway food was thrown at my back. I turned round to confront the yobs saying, "Watch it. I have your faces and I'll be reporting you to the school." They scattered like the cowards they were. But I wasn't out of the woods yet. Further down the street more youths were making unpleasant comments as somebody threw chips at me. "Fucking shit, I'll stab you in the heart " I heard as the owner of the voice vanished. Furious to be victimized in such a fashion I drove home wondering if it was time to clear out of Britain. The incident may have been captured on

CCTV, which would mean that the culprits would be identified but this was a long shot. The point I have to make is that this sort of anti-social behaviour is becoming more and more frequent. Nobody seems able to do much about it. As an authority figure merely trying to do your job you are on your own. You may have good intentions towards young people, but the way things are going all the idealism in the world can't make up for a widespread collapse in acceptable standards of behaviour. You may have started out as rebel yourself but inevitably the harsh lessons of life teach you to stand up for law and order. When I was young I might have been deeply resentful about authoritarian teachers and the general inflexibility of the surrounding society. Even so, I would never have challenged a teacher or any other authority figure in such a way. I was essentially a middle-class boy who believed in debate and discussion. I may have felt aggressive on occasions but I was self-disciplined and would never have hit anybody save in self-defence. These days though so many people are only too ready to resort to hitting out at random with no apparent thought for the consequences. The only remedy as far as I can see is to establish a new penal code that punishes law- breakers severely. The language of punishment is the only one that yobs and criminals understand. Most reasonable citizens are tired of putting up with vandalism, assault, petty crime of all sorts and want something to be done before the streets of Britain deteriorate into anarchy. Is anybody listening? A representative of the Old School rests his case.

"Lord do not forgive them for they know exactly what they do. Here endeth the lesson."

..............................................................................

# ABOUT THE AUTHOR

Joe Dullerson, a true Scot, comes from Glasgow, city of laughter and song. After education at Glasgow High School and Aberdeen University, he embarked on a non-career of dropout, supply teacher, failed academic and teacher of English as a foreign language. (Tefler)

He is a gonzo writer who demolishes myths and stereotypes with black and cutting humour. Still waiting for the Promised Land he is (like Clint Eastwood) a piano player over 55 who is the voice of a new, politically incorrect counter-culture. Despite the accuracy of Frank Zappa's comment that "You get nothing with a college diploma", he is an eternal optimist. Professor of Nihilism at the University of the Absurd, he is a provocative and innovative writer.

Lightning Source UK Ltd.
Milton Keynes UK
20 January 2011

166088UK00001B/133/A

9 781420 853346